"Can We Still Believe in the Rapture? is the most fair and balanced defense of the rapture in print today. Ed Hindson and Mark Hitchcock present a clear, concise, and credible defense of this amazing biblical doctrine. They give the believer a love for our Lord's coming. Don't miss it!"

Dr. Robert Jeffress, Pastor, First Baptist Church of Dallas, TX

"In an age where it is all too common to speak of the rapture as a recent idea that lacks biblical roots and leads to a lack of engagement with the world as it is, Mark Hitchcock and Ed Hindson take a close biblical look at the doctrine and the objections to it. This book is loaded with careful historical, biblical, and theological observations about pretribulationism. It is a book that should not be left behind!"

Darrell L. Bock, Executive Director for Cultural Engagement, Senior Research Professor of New Testament Studies, Dallas Theological Seminary

"I have read several helpful books on the rapture, but this one is at the top. Mark Hitchcock and Ed Hindson make a compelling exegetical, theological, and historical case for a pretribulational rapture. They also take on the best and most current arguments from those who oppose the pretribulational rapture view. Adherents of a pretrib rapture will be encouraged. Those who disagree will have to interact with the arguments in this book."

Michael J. Vlach, Professor of Theology, The Master's Seminary

"It's a vitally important question on a key topic for believers: Can we still believe in the rapture? I'm grateful for this substantive and biblical answer to the question and especially recommend that a new generation of Christians and pastors read and reflect upon the truths of this outstanding book."

Dr Jack Graham, Pastor, Prestonwood Baptist Church, Plano, TX

"Yes, we can still believe! Read this book with an open mind and you may also be convinced that you can believe in the rapture. When we believe in the rapture, our sense of urgency and our commitment to advancing the gospel increases greatly."

Dr. Ronnie Floyd, Senior Pastor, Cross Church, AR; President, National Day of Prayer; past president of Southern Baptist Convention

"The biblical doctrine concerning the rapture of the church has caused considerable debate and confusion among Christians. For many, when confusion ramps up, they are quick to back out, throw up their hands, and say, 'Who can really know?' I pray this is not your reaction. God's prophetic words exist to inform us, enthuse us, and motivate us regarding 'our blessed hope' (Titus 2:13). This book is sure to do just that. Hitchcock and Hindson carefully guide us through the biblical data, respond to today's popular criticisms, and help us to say with confidence, 'Yes, we can still believe in the rapture!'"

Mike Fabarez, Pastor, Compass Bible Church, Aliso Viejo, CA; host of Focal Point Radio Ministries

"This book provides a fair and balanced defense of classic, dispensational pretribulationism. Anyone interested in correctly understanding this position will benefit from this work."

Daniel L. Akin, President, Southeastern Baptist Theological Seminary

"Ed Hindson and Mark Hitchcock carefully walk us through what the Bible says about what could be the next great event on God's prophetic calendar. The early church was animated and purified by this 'blessed hope'—the joyous expectation of Jesus's return. Seeing that Jesus has yet to appear, this doctrine is even more relevant for us today in the twenty-first century. Now more than ever, every Christian and critic ought to consider carefully the simple and clear message of what God's Word has to say about the doctrine of the rapture."

Jack Hibbs, Senior Pastor, Calvary Chapel Chino Hills, CA; host of *Real Life* radio broadcast

"In today's church the blessed hope is increasingly a buried hope. Sadly the doctrine of the church's pretribulational rapture is being buried beneath an avalanche of caricatures and criticisms. Thankfully my friends Mark and Ed have come to this doctrine's rescue. Tunneling through history, digging through Scripture, and shoveling aside misunderstanding, they have uncovered for a new generation of Christians the biblical basis, historical justification, and practical impact of the blessed hope of Jesus imminent return for His church at the rapture. Can we still believe in the rapture? Yes we can, and yes we must!"

Philip De Courcy, Pastor, Kindred Community Church in Anaheim Hills, CA; Bible teacher on daily radio program *Know the Truth*

CAN WE STILL
BELIEVE IN THE
RAPTURE?

ED HINDSON &
MARK HITCHCOCK

HARVEST HOUSE PUBLISHERS
EUGENE, OREGON

CAN WE STILL BELIEVE IN THE RAPTURE?

Copyright © 2017 Ed Hindson and Mark Hitchcock
Published by Harvest House Publishers
Eugene, Oregon 97408
www.harvesthousepublishers.com

ISBN 978-0-7369-7189-8 (pbk.)
ISBN 978-0-7369-7190-4 (eBook)

Library of Congress Cataloging-in-Publication Data

Names: Hitchcock, Mark, 1959- author.
Title: Can we still believe in the rapture? / Mark Hitchcock and Ed Hindson.
Description: Eugene, Oregon : Harvest House Publishers, 2017. | Includes
    bibliographical references.
Identifiers: LCCN 2017019333 (print) | LCCN 2017041583 (ebook) | ISBN
    9780736971904 (ebook) | ISBN 9780736971898 (pbk.)
Subjects: LCSH: Rapture (Christian eschatology)
Classification: LCC BT887 (ebook) | LCC BT887 .H559 2017 (print) | DDC
    236/.9—dc23
LC record available at https://lccn.loc.gov/2017019333

Printed in the United States of America

19 20 21 22 23 24 25 / BP-SK / 10 9 8 7 6 5 4 3

To *"all who love his appearing"*
and for whom "there will be a crown of righteousness."

2 TIMOTHY 4:8

Contents

The Purpose for This Book

One of the clearest teachings in the New Testament is the promise of the rapture. Yet it remains one of the most debated issues in Christian theology. Virtually every Christian denomination affirms its belief in the eventual return of Jesus Christ. However, beyond this basic affirmation there exists a wide variety of opinions with regard to when and how Christ will return. And some have even questioned the whole idea of whether Christ will rapture believers at all.

Our purpose in writing this book is to examine the biblical doctrine of the rapture, answer objections that are often raised against it, and provide a reasonable basis of discussion within the context of evangelical theology. In carrying out this objective, we have endeavored to maintain a tone that is respectful and engaging. Our hope is to encourage a positive and thoughtful approach to this often-controversial topic. Our goal is to instill a love for Christ, a respect for His bride, and a confidence in the "blessed hope" of His return (Titus 2:13).

We have worked together at a distance with the editorial assistance of Dillon Burroughs and Michael W. Herbert. We both serve on the executive board of the Pre-Trib Research Center in Dallas, Texas. We are also both actively engaged in ministry and education—Mark at

Edmond Bible Church in Edmond, Oklahoma, and Dallas Theological Seminary, and Ed at *The King Is Coming* telecast and Liberty
University. In these capacities we have seen the hope, help, and joy
that the message of the rapture brings to the hearts of believers everywhere. It is our prayer that this study will inform your mind, bless
your heart, and stir your soul with a renewed love for Christ and a
desire for His coming.

Ed Hindson and Mark Hitchcock

CHAPTER 1

Rapture Under Attack

*The rapture is a racket. Whether prescribing a violent
script for Israel or survivalism in the United States,
this theology distorts God's vision for the world.*[1]

BARBARA R. ROSSING, *THE RAPTURE EXPOSED*

So begins one of the more popular attacks on the pretribulation
view in recent years. Rossing, like others holding this perspective, claims a pretribulational view of the rapture fosters escapism,
replaces peacemaking with a glorification of war, and celebrates the
wrath of God. She goes on to claim:

> This theology is not biblical. We are not Raptured off
> the earth, nor is God. No, God has come to live in the
> world through Jesus. God created the world, God loves
> the world, and God will never leave the world behind![2]

Such an opinion can hardly be reconciled with the biblical statement that "earth and heaven fled away, and no place was found for
them" (Revelation 20:11) because "the first heaven and the first earth
passed away" (Revelation 21:1).

Others accuse those who hold a pretribulation view as showing
racial discrimination. Hank Hanegraaff claims:

The good news for Jews is that LaHaye believes that on the basis of their race they have a divine right to the land of Palestine. The bad news is that, as a direct result of the crucifixion of Christ, twenty-first-century Jews will soon die in an Armageddon that will make the Nazi Holocaust pale by comparison.[3]

Hanegraaff later adds:

[The] theory of two peoples of God has had chilling consequences not only for Jews, but for Palestinian Arabs as well…Such unbiblical notions put Christian Zionists in the untenable position of condoning the displacement of Palestinian Christians from their homeland in order to facilitate an occupation based on unbelief and racial affiliation.[4]

If a person were to believe such criticisms, Christians who interpret the Bible as including a pretribulation rapture are unbiblical, anti-Semitic, survivalists, have a distorted view of God, are against caring for God's creation, and are racist! All this from simply believing what the Bible clearly states—that "we who are still alive and are left will be caught up together with them in the clouds to meet the Lord in the air. And so we will be with the Lord forever" (1 Thessalonians 4:17 NIV).

Why the Divide?

Unfortunately, these accusations come primarily from Christians rather than those who claim no religious affiliation. Why has there been such animosity among some believers regarding Christ's coming?

Some of the most vocal objections to the idea of the rapture have come from those who lack a clear, exegetically based understanding of it in the first place. They become easily confused by statements like " The word *rapture* is not in the Bible"; "Christians have always suffered tribulation"; "No one believed in a pretrib rapture before 1830"; "The Bible doesn't teach two second comings or two last trumpets."[5]

1. Naïve Acceptance

Christians of all types initially tend to uncritically accept whatever theological ideas happen to be taught in the church fellowship where they first came to the faith. This includes a wide variety of doctrinal beliefs, including those relating to eschatology. Some people believe in the rapture simply because that is what they were taught early in their spiritual experience. Naïve acceptance of any doctrine leaves sincere believers vulnerable to critical objections to their faith that they are unprepared to answer.

2. Theological Ignorance

Biblical truth is anchored in a theological context drawn from Scripture. Without a proper understanding of that context, some Christians are inconsistent in certain elements of their faith. Specific details of eschatology are accepted or dismissed with little or no understanding of a biblical, theological context. As a result, many Christians become easily confused by the basic elements of any serious discussion of biblical prophecies about the future.

3. Popular Influence

Unfortunately, many evangelicals in general are influenced by the views of popular speakers, teachers, and writers. Attracted to the general ideas of a popular teacher, they tend to embrace the teacher's eschatology as well. This happens with various prophetic views of all kinds, whether the teacher is David Jeremiah, John MacArthur, John Hagee, R.C. Sproul, John Piper, or Tim Keller.[6]

4. Unexpected Questions

Many people struggle with questions about Bible prophecy that are raised by others around them. These questions can range across a wide spectrum: Why isn't the word *rapture* in the Bible? Isn't the concept of a pretribulation rapture a relatively new idea? If all believers are raptured *after* the tribulation, who will populate Jesus's millennial kingdom? If it's true that the church replaces Israel, then what happens to God's promise never to forsake Israel? These questions can be unsettling for those who aren't familiar with the prophetic portions of Scripture and Bible prophecy in general.

5. Difficult Challenges

Some believers abandon any attempt to resolve the challenges that are raised when they study eschatology. They simply decide it will all "pan out" in the end, and they may even halfheartedly claim to be "pan-millennial." Because some interpretive details of eschatology are indeed challenging, even some pastors are unwilling to do the hard work of sorting them all out.

6. Paradigm Shift

Some overreact to the questions they are unprepared to answer and make a complete paradigm shift in their thinking. Instead of formulating a clear exegetical understanding of the biblical text, they simply adopt an opposite view. Challenged by a few questions they are not prepared to answer, they uncritically assume an opposite view must be correct. Too many times people do this without considering the ramifications of the new idea they have adopted.

7. Adversarial Responses

Whenever people drastically change their theological views, it becomes very tempting for them to demonize the view they previously held by denouncing it with a harsh, adversarial response. Thus, former Catholics, Charismatics, Baptists, and Presbyterians often become the harshest critics of a given group or teaching. The same is true with regard to eschatology. Those who once held a pretrib view of the rapture often become virtually hateful in their rejection of that view—even to the point of bitter sarcasm when referring to the rapture itself despite the fact it is clearly taught in the Bible. All views of eschatology (except full preterism) believe there will be a rapture of living believers and a simultaneous resurrection of dead believers. The only real difference between the views is the matter of the *timing* of the rapture.

All too often, discussions about eschatology shed more heat than light. Angry expressions, pejorative reactions, and hateful remarks prevent any serious interaction with those who hold opposing views. Mocking skewers and condemns, and fails to redeem. The intent of some is to vilify rather than inform. They make hideous and outrageous remarks about other believers' views and thus fail the test of loving one another as Christ loved the church (see Ephesians 5:25).

In reality, all true Christians believe God will win in the end! Pretribulationalists believe He will win by rapturing the church, converting Israel, condemning the world, fulfilling the millennial promises, and ushering in the eternal state. The other eschatological views more or less see the same end results, but they take different routes to get there. For example, mid- and posttribulationalists believe God will preserve the church through part or all of the tribulation, and then the rapture and other eschatological events will follow. Postmillennialists believe the church is converted "Israel" and that they are bringing in the millennium now. Amillennialists believe all these things will happen, mostly in a spiritual sense, at the end of the church era preceding eternity.

Each view of eschatology contains elements of truth but applies them in a different manner. Pretribulationalists urge believers to be prepared because Jesus could return at any time. Mid- and post-tribulationalists urge believers to be prepared, if necessary, to suffer for their faith until Jesus comes. Postmillennialists insist we have a responsibility to transform the world as long as we are still here. Amillennialists remind us that heaven is our ultimate destiny. Each of these concerns is biblical, practical, and a vital part of evangelical Christianity.

In our growing information age, it is often the loudest voices that demand the most attention. From political debates to viral videos, communication shouts messages more than in past generations. When it comes to views concerning the end times, several "new" voices have popularized loud—and sometimes bold—attacks against the pretribulation view as part of promoting their own "brand" or end-times teachings. A brief Internet search on the "pre-trib rapture," for example, will lead to many results proclaiming, "How the Pre-Trib Rapture Is a Deception," or, "The False Doctrine of the Pre-Trib Rapture."

Attacks on the Pretrib Rapture View

Finding information on the topic is not a problem; the problem is discovering which information is helpful in the discussion. In both academic and popular writings, four areas of attack on the pretribulational rapture view have emerged as the most common:

1. There is no rapture (Jesus will restore all things someday, but not in a specific rapture).

2. The preterist view (the "rapture" occurred during the first century).

3. The minimalist view (the rapture is coming, but we don't know when).

4. The posttribulation/New Reformation view (one rapture at the end of the tribulation).

Let's take a look at each of these four arguments to discuss their strengths and weaknesses.

The "No Rapture" View

I (Ed) was listening to an amillennial pastor friend preach a message on the second coming. He concluded with the words, "And so we see that there never will be a rapture. All we have to look forward to is trouble, trouble, and more trouble!" At which point his congregation let out a loud moan. I was tempted to jump up and shout, "Therefore comfort one another with these words" (see 1 Thessalonians 4:18). Afterward I reminded him that there has to be a time when the dead are raised and the living are "caught up" (the rapture). We simply disagree on the *timing* of the event, not the *fact* that it will happen.

Despite the Bible's clear teaching—in which Jesus said, "If I go and prepare a place for you, I will come again and receive you to Myself, that where I am, there you may be also" (John 14:3)—many who do not believe in a pretribulational rapture assume there will be no rapture at all. This view, held by many in the United Kingdom, is well represented by British New Testament scholar N.T. Wright. Known for writing both academic and popular books about Jesus, he noted in an article entitled "Farewell to the Rapture":

> The American obsession with the second coming of Jesus—especially with distorted interpretations of it—continues unabated. Seen from my side of the Atlantic, the phenomenal success of the Left Behind books appears puzzling, even bizarre. Few in the U.K. hold the belief on which the popular series of novels is based: that there will be a literal "rapture" in which believers will be snatched up to heaven, leaving empty cars crashing on freeways and kids coming home from school only to find that their parents have been taken to be with Jesus while they have been "left behind." This pseudo-theological version of Home Alone has reportedly frightened many children into some kind of (distorted) faith.[7]

He continues with a brief commentary that provides an alternative view of the end of times, suggesting, "The New Testament, building on ancient biblical prophecy, envisages that the creator God will remake heaven and earth entirely, affirming the goodness of the old Creation but overcoming its mortality and corruptibility."[8]

Rapture passages such as 1 Thessalonians 4:13-18 are limited to borrowing metaphors from Old Testament passages to speak of the transformation that believers will experience at the end of time. Wright further emphasizes Jesus did not speak of His return in such vivid ways, but suggests only Paul did.[9] However, Paul clearly affirmed, "This we say to you by the word of the Lord" (verse 15)!

The return of Jesus serves as a foundation of Christian belief. Early Christian statements such as the Nicene Creed offered a very limited focus on the end times, such as belief in "the resurrection of the dead, and the life of the world to come."[10] However, the church has long held to an understanding of Jesus one day returning to this world as He promised in John 14:1-3. Believers often argue regarding the timing of this coming to rapture or take His people to be with Him, but they still agree the Scriptures teach that He *will* come.

One of the earliest Christian writings outside of the New Testament is the *Didache*, a Greek word that means "teachings." The *Didache* includes a compilation of early church doctrines and was most likely written between 70–180. It says this regarding the future: "Be vigilant over your life; let your lamps not be extinguished, or your loins ungirded, but be prepared, for you know not the hour in which our Lord will come" (16:1). Though not explicitly pretribulational in nature, the passage clearly affirms a view in which the Lord will return at any moment.

Also, how else are readers to understand Paul's words regarding this future "mystery" that "we will not all sleep, but we will all be changed—in a moment, in the twinkling of an eye, at the last trumpet; for the trumpet will sound, and the dead will be raised imperishable, and we will be changed" (1 Corinthians 15:51-52)? The end of time includes more than restoring all things—it includes a transformation of believers living on the earth at the time of Christ's coming.

The Preterist View

The preterist view holds that most, or all, of the main New Testament prophetic passages were fulfilled in the first century. Within this view are full preterists and partial preterists. Full preterists contend *all* the prophecies of the New Testament have already been fulfilled, including the second coming and resurrection of believers. Few hold this particular view of preterism.[11]

Usually when someone says he or she holds a preterist view, they are referring to *partial* preterism. R.C. Sproul, a well-known adherent of this view, says it "places many or all eschatological events in the past, especially during the destruction of Jerusalem in AD 70."[12] This includes the belief that prophecies regarding Jesus coming in a cloud referred to the destruction of Jerusalem in the first century, that Nero was the beast in Revelation, and that the evil "Babylon" of eschatology was actually Jerusalem.[13]

Most who hold this view also argue the book of Revelation was written in the AD 60s rather than the traditional date of AD 95. If true, this would more easily allow the prophecies of Revelation to fit first-century events that took place a few years later. However, the best scholarship continues to support the traditional view of the later date of Revelation, a fact that holds strong negative consequences for those seeking to justify a preterist view.

Hanegraaff also holds to a preterist view, which influences his popular book *The Apocalypse Code* as well as his *Last Disciple* novel series. However, many of the concepts taught in this theory fail if Revelation was written after AD 70. Norman Geisler's review of Hanegraaff's work observes:

> ...as even partial preterist Kenneth Gentry admits, there is "strong external witness" that John wrote after AD

70 during Domitian's reign (260). Indeed, the earliest witness (Irenaeus) knew Polycarp (1st cent), the disciple of the apostle John. With him there is an unbroken series of early Fathers who held that John wrote after AD 70 including Irenaeus (2nd cent), Victorinus (3rd cent), and Eusebius (4th cent.). The significance of this cannot be overstated. For the early view of John does not destroy the futurist view (that the Tribulation is after AD 70). However, the late view totally destroys the preterist since it is referring to the Tribulation as yet future after AD 70.[14]

Both the popular and academic arguments that suggest the rapture and associated events occurred during the first century AD struggle when evaluated by the facts of history. Though Jesus did speak of prophetic events that occurred near His time, He also spoke of yet-unfilled prophecies that still require investigation by readers today: the gospel "preached in the whole world as a testimony to all nations," a time of great tribulation worse than anything the world will ever see; the sign of the Son of Man coming in the clouds with power and glory; the gathering of all nations for the judgment (Matthew 24:14 NIV, 21, 30; 25:31-32).

The Minimalist View

The minimalist view refers to the growing idea among many evangelical Christians that Jesus will return one day, but we don't know when. Some further contend we *cannot* know when, arguing that even Jesus does not know the day or the hour (Matthew 24:36). Some holding this view jokingly suggest they are pan-tribulationists or pan-millennialists, saying, "It will all pan out in the end." Often people retreat to this approach as a reaction against failed attempts to date the rapture or identify the antichrist.

The weakness with this view is not its inaccuracy, but its lack of concern for the Bible's clear teachings about the end times. Consider how much of Scripture is prophetic in nature. Of the Bible's 31,124 verses, 8,352 of them include predictions. This is 27 percent of the entire Bible! In the New Testament, one out of every 30 verses has to do with future events. If more than one-fourth of the Bible touches on the future, Christians should have a high level of concern for better understanding what those passages say and how they apply to today.

There are three primary reasons people adopt this minimalist approach. First, some have grown tired of the fear-based content that appears in many prophetic books, films, and other forms of media. The desire to "feel good" and focus on the positive has led many in today's churches to neglect the study of biblical prophecy. Because they want to emphasize only the positive aspects of the gospel, they avoid what they wrongly perceive as the negative message of Bible prophecy.

Second, minimalists want to avoid controversy. Because the study of prophecy has often included debates regarding various views of the end times, a growing number of evangelicals simply avoid the discussion altogether so they can avoid the debates.

Third, for some people, the concerns of this world (Matthew 13:22) have taken priority over the pursuit of spiritual maturity. This includes those who fulfill the words of 2 Timothy 4:3-4: "The time will come when they will not endure sound doctrine; but *wanting* to have their ears tickled, they will accumulate for themselves teachers in accordance to their own desires, and will turn away their ears from the truth and will turn aside to myths." Spiritual growth is often difficult, as is the study of prophecy. However, Scripture encourages us to study to show ourselves approved (2 Timothy 2:15). Romans 12:2 challenges believers to "not be conformed to this world, but be transformed by the renewing of your mind." Bible prophecy is not written to *scare* us but rather to *prepare* us for the Lord's return.

A Pew Research study regarding US Christians' views on the

return of Jesus offered some interesting insights. First, 47 percent agreed they believe Jesus will "definitely" or "probably" return to earth in the next 40 years. However, another surprising insight is that 14 percent said they did not know if Jesus would return during this time, while 38 percent agreed Jesus will "definitely" or "probably" not return in the next 40 years.[15] Over half of American Christians (self-identified Christians, not all Americans) either don't know or don't think Jesus is coming back any time soon. The actions of these American views are often reflected in views of the end times, with more people simply unconcerned about Jesus's return or its timing.

The Repopularized Posttribulation View

The posttribulation view generally holds that the second coming of Jesus takes place at the end of the seven-year tribulation period. However, a growing number of scholars who do not hold to a literal seven-year tribulation are now preferring to call the position "historic premillennialism."[16] This view often emphasizes the fact that believers in Christ will remain on earth during periods of great upheaval and judgment. While this view has often had supporters, two factors have contributed to the increased popularity of the posttribulation view in recent years.

First, a growing number of believers feel persecuted. There are organizations that keep track of the countries in which Christians are persecuted. In 2016, for the first time ever, the United States appeared on the list.[17] In the past decade, the number of lawsuits, legal cases, and headlines involving religious liberty issues has grown exponentially. Combined with the increased persecution of Christians in other regions, such as North Africa and the Middle East, many Christians feel as if we could already be experiencing the persecution that will come in the last days.

The second factor is the growing resurgence of Reformed theology in evangelical circles. Both traditional Reformed institutions and Reformed beliefs within other denominational groups have increased in recent years, perhaps reaching a high point in 2017 with the 500th anniversary of the Protestant Reformation. While many of the beliefs affirmed by the Protestant Reformation and its theologians have been beneficial to the church, some accept the entire system of Reformed theology without a careful analysis of its parts. In other words, some who accept Reformed beliefs regarding soteriology (the doctrine of salvation) often accept Reformed eschatology without question.

This view has become more popular due to the influence of some well-known evangelical teachers. For example, Al Mohler and John Piper have shaped the thinking of many conservative Christians. Wayne Grudem's popular *Systematic Theology* textbook, which is used in many Christian colleges and seminaries, has introduced many to this view, while Mike Bickle has influenced many charismatic Christians.[18]

Popular Misconceptions

Even careful scholars have participated in spreading misconceptions in their criticisms of certain rapture views. This is true of all eschatological views. Pretribulationalists are accused of an escapist mentality that appeals to those who are unwilling to suffer for their faith.[19] Posttribulationalists are castigated as "preppers" hiding out and awaiting the tribulation. Postmillennialists are viewed as naïve dreamers who are detached from reality. Amillennialists are seen as so heavenly minded they are no earthly good.

Each of these misconceptions is based on popular myths that circulate among Christians in general. They spring from glaring misconceptions of biblical teaching. For example, some people actually thought that if Hillary Clinton won the presidential election in 2016, she would persecute Christians and usher in the tribulation. Others speculated that if she won, the rapture would have to take place immediately. Still others asked if there was any possibility that Donald Trump might be the "last trump"!

Often eschatological "urban myths" (*eschatomania* or *eschatophobia*) arise from attempts to identify current events with biblical prophecies. Some serious scholars have admitted they were turned off to biblical prophecy because of unsubstantiated speculations that did not come true. For example, during World War II, Japan was often viewed as the "army from the east" (see Revelation 9:14-19). Later, popularists suggested it was China. During the Cold War era, Russia was often viewed as the perpetrator of war in the Middle East—an idea that is now being revived. With the rise of Islamic extremism, some have suggested the antichrist will be a Muslim. And frequently, candidates who run for president of the United States are believed to be the prospective antichrist.

Is the Rapture a Scare Tactic?

There are some who say that promoting the belief that Jesus will return at any moment is a scare tactic. Some would even label such an approach as spiritual abuse, associating every high-pressure evangelistic appeal as the direct result of the pretribulation rapture view. Speculations about cars and airplanes crashing due to the rapture of their drivers and pilots are used to criticize the pretrib view when, in reality, the same problems would be present no matter what one's view of the timing of the rapture. Even if the rapture were to occur at the end of time, one cannot assume everyone will be a pedestrian at that moment.

Yet the question is not whether someone is scared by any particular view of the end times, but ultimately whether it is true. Norman Geisler suggests, "*First*, there is nothing wrong with fear as a motive if it is based in truth...*Second*, most arguments for pretribulationalism are not based on fear. *Third*, misuse does not bar use. That is, even some arguments being incorrectly cast...does not invalidate the proper use of the argument in particular nor pretribulationalism in general."[20]

All too often people object to a specific view of eschatology by raising a series of what are known as straw man arguments. The straw man fallacy is the creation of an intentionally weakened, distorted, exaggerated, or false version of an opponent's arguments and attacking them accordingly. As a result, the critic fails to "see" what they don't want to see—even if it is clearly there.

In this book, we will look at the abundance of evidence in support of the pretribulation view of the rapture. And while it's true that Bible prophecy reveals information that gives us reason to be concerned about what lies ahead for our world, it can also have a tremendously positive effect.

The Positive Effects of Pretrib Rapture Teaching

The late Tim LaHaye was fond of pointing out that "historically, belief in the any-moment-coming of Christ has three vital effects on Christians and their churches."[21] He notes the following three positive and beneficial results of the pretribulation rapture view.

1. It Produces Holy Living in an Unholy Society

Believing Jesus can return at any time can certainly inspire a higher level of accountability in a person's life. And isn't this precisely what Scripture teaches? When Peter wrote to some church elders in his first letter, he said, "When the Chief Shepherd appears, you will receive the unfading crown of glory" (1 Peter 5:4). He adds in verses 6-7, "Therefore humble yourselves under the mighty hand of God, that He may exalt you at the proper time, casting all your anxiety on Him, because He cares for you." Believers are called to humble themselves and to anticipate the rewards they will one day receive when Jesus, our "Chief Shepherd," appears.

In 1 John 3:3 we also find mention of the appearance of Jesus: "Everyone who has this hope fixed on Him purifies himself, just as He is pure." The believer's anticipation of being with Christ, whether at the rapture or in death, rightly causes a desire to live a pure and holy life.

What should concern us most is a lackadaisical, lukewarm Christianity that doesn't take seriously the possibility Christ may come soon (2 Peter 3:3-4). We are to be holy as He is holy (1 Peter 1:15). Further, 2 Peter 3:10-11 adds a fitting rhetorical question concerning the believer's holiness in light of Christ's possible-at-any-moment return: "The day of the Lord will come like a thief. The heavens will disappear with a roar; the elements will be destroyed by fire, and the earth and everything done in it will be laid bare. Since everything will be destroyed in this way, what kind of people ought you to be? You ought to live holy and godly lives" (NIV).

2. It Produces an Evangelistic Church

The early church was an evangelistic church. On the day the church began, 3,000 people were added to their number (Acts 2:41). The first written summary about the church in Jerusalem notes the Lord added to their number *daily* those who were being saved (Acts 2:47).

Those who believe Jesus will rapture believers to be with Him—and that He could do so at any moment—are strongly motivated to share their faith with family members, friends, and anyone else they can. Some say this is a weakness of the pretribulation view, but the fact is, Scripture commands all Christians to evangelize. Regardless of whether or not we hold to the pretribulation view, we are called to share Christ with all. We are to share Paul's attitude, made evident in his declaration, "I am not ashamed of the gospel, for it is the power of God for salvation to everyone who believes" (Romans 1:16).

3. It Encourages Believers to Develop a Vision for World Missions

In addition to producing an evangelistic church, the belief that Jesus could return at any moment encourages a vision for world missionary outreach. Note the final earthly words of Jesus Christ: "Go therefore and make disciples of all the nations, baptizing them in the name of the Father and the Son and the Holy Spirit, teaching them to observe all that I commanded you; and lo, I am with you always, even to the end of the age" (Matthew 28:19-20).

There may be a strong correlation between the missionary activity of the first century and the global missionary movement of the past century. In both contexts, a growing awareness that Jesus could return at any moment has led to many individuals to travel so they can share the good news of Christ. And if they cannot travel, they support those who can.

Norman Geisler notes:

> If one believes his time is limited and Christ may come at any moment, then he will have more of a sense of urgency about evangelism. This, of course, is not to say that there is no sense of urgency in the other views for everyone is going to die and some will die at any moment. But there is a far greater sense of urgency if one believes it could be our last opportunity to reach anyone at any moment. It is no coincidence that many of the modern missionary movements (William Carey, David Livingston, and Adoniram Judson) and evangelistic efforts (Billy Sunday, D.L. Moody, and Billy Graham) were headed by premillennialists.[22]

One could add to this list such leading pretribulational pastors as David Jeremiah, John MacArthur, Charles Stanley, Tony Evans, Jack Graham, Robert Jeffress, Chuck Swindoll, Philip De Courcy, Johnny Hunt, Ronnie Floyd, Donald Perkins, Chuck Smith, Jack Hibbs, Skip Heitzig, Mike Fabarez, and Greg Laurie.

Attacks on the rapture have grown in intensity and number. In *Can We Still Believe in the Rapture?* we'll help you understand the fallacies inherent in these attacks, present helpful information from today's best research, and explain what God's Word teaches on this topic. You'll also discover the benefits of living with the biblical perspective that Christ could return any day—even today!

CHAPTER 2

Separating Fact from Fiction

There are several reasons why prophecy has a bad reputation...due to many false predictions by well-meaning but misguided souls.[1]

ERWIN W. LUTZER

Most of us would like to believe that Jesus is coming within our lifetime. Yet even as we anticipate the Lord's return, we need to be aware that eschatological excitement and prophetic panic go hand in hand. Every time there is a "blood moon" or war heats up in the Middle East, there are a number of "prophetic panhandlers" who assure us this is the Big One. Despite the church's twenty-one centuries of struggling to carefully and correctly understand biblical prophecy, contemporary speculators often claim to have the last days and Christ's return all figured out—some to the very day!

Eschatological speculation is especially prevalent among new believers. They are excited about their newfound faith and the promise of Christ's return. They sincerely believe the Bible, but they often want to make it say more than it really says. They especially want to believe that they are living in the last days and that current events are of great prophetic significance. The problem is that some Christians are eager to read prophecies about the future through the eyes of the present. The results have been a host of miscalculated guesses based on faulty presumptions.

There is certainly nothing wrong with Christians taking seriously the doctrine of the second coming. Scripture says that one day Christ will literally return to the earth to vindicate the church and judge the world. We may differ among ourselves on *when* and *how* He will return, but we remain convinced He will return as He promised.

However, we must exercise discernment when we deal with the teachings about the imminence of Christ's return. Yes, it's correct to believe that He could come at any moment. While there are exceptions to this, most evangelical Christians are expecting Him to return soon. While this hope gives the church great comfort and expectation, this anticipation can easily lead to excessive speculation. Classic examples of this have included Edgar Whisenant's book *88 Reasons Why the Rapture Will Be in 1988*[2]; a Korean sect's newspaper ads predicting October 22, 1992, as the date of Christ's return[3]; the widespread concerns over Y2K and J.M. Hile's *Timeline 2000*[4]; Harold Camping's infamous "Judgment Day" prediction of May 21, 2011[5]; the so-called Mayan calendar doomsday—December 21, 2012[6]; and the four blood moons, which occurred on April 15, 2014; October 8. 2014; April 4, 2014; and September 27, 2015.[7]

Everything Old Is New Again

New believers are often quick to accept such predictions without question because they just don't know better. Many of them have a limited knowledge of the Bible, let alone biblical prophecy. In most cases they tend to believe whatever end-times position is promoted in the church where they received Christ. "After all," they theorize, "if my church is right about salvation, it must be right about prophecy too." Even pastors with some theological training have been known to fall for whatever happens to be the latest eschatological scam.

The twentieth century abounded with prophetic speculations that were inaccurate or never came true. For example, there have been endless attempts to identify key international leaders as being the antichrist of the last days:

Kaiser Wilhelm

This German leader's title meant "Caesar," and he intended to conquer all of Europe and reunite the old Roman Empire. But in the end, he lost World War I and failed to fulfill the expectations of prophetic speculators.

Benito Mussolini

The Italian strong man from Rome rose to power after World War I and was soon tagged as the coming antichrist long before World War II began. After all, people reasoned, he was in Rome, where he might form an alliance with the pope to revive the ancient Roman Empire.

Adolph Hitler

Hitler has come to represent the ultimate personification of evil. He persecuted and murdered six million Jews and tried to conquer all of Europe. During World War II he formed an alliance with Mussolini, but eventually both were defeated and destroyed.

Joseph Stalin

This atheistic leader of the Soviet Union may have been an ally during World War II, but it was an uneasy alliance at best. He was leader over Russia during the opening years of the Cold War and was responsible for executing millions of his own people.

Nikita Khrushchev

This outspoken, shoe-pounding, large, bald man of the Soviet Union threatened to bury us all. But he was wrong.

John F. Kennedy

Remarkably, anti-Catholic fundamentalists in the 1960s believed Kennedy was a top candidate for becoming the antichrist. They were sure he was going to deceive the American public, form an alliance with the pope, and conquer the world.

Mikhail Gorbachev

Extremists pointed to the birthmark on his forehead and asked if it might be the "mark of the beast." They thought his offers of peace, *perestroika*, and *glasnost* were too good to be true and that he could not be trusted.

Ronald Wilson Reagan

Yes, even the darling of the New Right was targeted as a candidate for the antichrist because his three names contained six letters each, which some connected with the number 666 (see Revelation 13:18).

Saddam Hussein

Some speculators suggested that the Iraqi leader would sign a peace treaty with Israel only to break it later and renew his hostilities toward the Promised Land.

Bill Clinton

Some people suggested Clinton was the antichrist and Al Gore was the false prophet of New Age religion.

Other candidates for prophetic speculators have included Henry Kissinger, Margaret Thatcher, Boris Yeltsin, George W. Bush, Hillary Clinton, and Barack Obama.[8] The problem with such identifications is that they are always tentative and viewed through the cultural and political lens of the times. Identifications that now seem ludicrous once held great popular appeal.

A Nearsighted View of the Future

When it comes to interpreting Bible prophecy, one of the more common problems is the tendency for people to view biblical predictions through the eyes of their own personal experience. The Germans call this a *zeitgeist*, a current mood or response to certain existing conditions.[9] Thus, the great temptation for those who attempt to interpret prophecy is to move from the biblical *facts* to their own *assumptions* and *speculations*. As they view the future through the eyes of the present, their speculations can end up seeming like real possibilities.

The tragedy of all this is that instead of rejecting prophetic speculation for what it is, many Christians are often duped by it. What's more, those who attempt to guess the date of Christ's coming and determine the identity of the antichrist are claiming to know more than the authors of Scripture. Daniel Mitchell, professor of theology at Liberty University, has said, "Speculating on the date of Christ's return not only breeds bad theology...it is the original sin all over again—trying to know as much as God."[10]

The expectation that the rapture could happen at *any moment* has been a source of hope and comfort to believers since the days of the apostles. Any apparent delay is not due to God's indecision, but to the fact that He has not let us in on the date!

In the meantime, we are admonished to "stand firm" and hold onto the doctrine of the apostles (2 Thessalonians 2:15) that we might be strengthened "in every good deed and word" (verse 17 NIV). Thus Paul's instruction is the same as that of Jesus, who told us to watch, stay ready, and keep serving until He returns (Matthew 24:42-46).

Here is a key principle to keep in mind at all times: Be sure to distinguish the *facts* of prophecy from the interpretive *assumptions* you draw and the *speculations* you make. While we would all like to believe that our Lord will return during our lifetime, it is presumptuous to assume that we are the terminal generation—even if all the signs seem to point that way. Jesus could come today, but then again, He may not come for several more years or even decades. The timing of the return is up to God the Father.

One of the most difficult tasks with regard to interpreting God's Word has been that of determining how we should understand the prophecies about the end times. Alan Bandy and Benjamin Merkle point out that an overemphasis on contemporary application often causes prophetic interpreters to skip over the task of discerning what the prophetic text *meant* in the first place.[11] First, we must remember that the people of Jesus's day misunderstood many of the predictions about His first coming. Therefore, we must not presume that we have figured out all the details about His second coming. Second, we must guard against the temptation to read *future* prophecy through the eyes of the *present*.

Unfortunately, unguarded speculation continues to prevail. Some of the wildest possible scenarios have received surprisingly widespread support. Prophetic speculation is often the strongest in reaction to perceived external threats. This is especially true today in regard to Islamic extremism. New theories about the last days have abounded since 9/11, and this includes identifying the antichrist as coming from Muslim roots.[12]

Guidelines for Understanding Prophecy

A wide variety of speculations have arisen with regard to the date of the rapture, the identity of the antichrist, and the beginning of the Battle of Armageddon. In our effort to make sense of all of this, we suggest a simple paradigm:

Facts

These are the clearly stated *prophetic propositions*. Christ will return for His own (John 14:13-17); those who are believers will be raptured (1 Thessalonians 4:13-17); there will be a time of great trouble on the earth at the end of the age (Matthew 24:21-22); the final conflict will be won by Christ (Revelation 19:11-21); He will judge the lost (Revelation 20:11-15); He will reign on the earth as well as in heaven (Revelation 20–22). These facts are clearly stated in the Bible.

Interpretations

The facts of prophecy tell us only so much, and no more. What's more, we are warned not to add to or subtract from what God has revealed in His prophetic Word (Revelation 22:18-19). That is, we should not try to make the Bible say more than it does, or less than it does. This challenge faces every biblical interpreter. Our *interpretive assumptions* need to be based upon a proper exegesis of Scripture. If our interpretive assumptions are correct, they will lead to valid conclusions, but if not, they may lead to ridiculous speculations. For example, matters such as the resurrection of the body, the length of Christ's earthly reign, or the literal nature of heaven all depend on one's interpretive assumptions.

Speculations

These are *calculated guesses* based upon interpretive assumptions. In many cases, there may be no clear factual basis for these. They are simply educated (or uneducated) guesses. These often include speculations about America's place in Bible prophecy, the identity of the antichrist, the combatants in the end-time wars, the mark of the beast, whether cars and airplanes will crash when Christian drivers and pilots are taken up at the time of the rapture. The greatest danger of all in handling Bible prophecy is to assume that our speculations are true and proclaim them as facts.[13]

The time has come when serious students of biblical prophecy must be clear about what is fact, what is assumption, and what is speculation. For example, just because a war erupts in the Middle East does not necessarily mean that war will lead to Armageddon. More specifically, consider the prophecy of the two witnesses in Revelation 11:3-13. The biblical *facts* state that they will prophesy in Jerusalem ("the city where our Lord was crucified") for 1,260 days, be killed, resurrected back to life, and raptured to heaven. Interpretive *assumptions* deal with the timing of these events, the identity of the two witnesses, the nature of the celebration that follows their death, and whether their resurrections and raptures are literal or figurative. Beyond these matters, *speculations* include whether satellite television transmissions may be involved in making it possible for people worldwide to see the two witnesses lying dead in the street for three-and-a-half days while people everywhere celebrate their demise and send presents to one another.

The issue at stake is not whether we can win an argument, but whether we can properly interpret biblical prophecy. In our attempts to do so, we must all clearly distinguish between the biblical facts, our interpretive assumptions, and our personal speculations—which exist in *all* the prophetic views. The greatest *fact* of all is that we who are in Christ have the hope of eternal life. As the apostle Peter said, "In his great mercy he has given us new birth into a living hope…into an inheritance that can never perish, spoil or fade. This inheritance is kept in heaven for you…ready to be revealed in the last time" (1 Peter 1:3-5).

Taking Prophecy Seriously

Whatever a specific believer's eschatological preference may be, as a whole, we as evangelical Christians take seriously the biblical prophecies about the end times and the return of Christ. Many of us believe we are living in the end times—when the world will be plunged into a series of cataclysmic wars that will rock the planet. However, just because we believe such events will happen does not mean we want to hasten them. But we do take the ominous warnings of Scripture seriously. In past centuries, when Christians talked about the end of the world, people often laughed at them because the destruction of the entire planet seemed inconceivable. But today, both Christians and secularists realize a catastrophe of that magnitude is well within the realm of possibility.[14]

In recent years, even the secular community has come to realize that we are approaching a potential cataclysmic disaster of "biblical proportions."[15] Concerns over global warming, air and water pollution, the destruction of the protective ozone layer, population explosion, and the general instability of the earth's crust have all been cited as serious problems that could affect the future of life on this planet.

The Bible warns that "the day of the Lord will come just like a thief in the night" (1 Thessalonians 5:1-2). It will be a dramatic event that will catch the world unprepared. Humankind has continually and irrevocably demonstrated that it cannot bring a permanent and lasting peace to this world. Every human effort at peace has been short-lived at best and ultimately destined to failure. At the time of the end, when the stakes are the highest, the greatest attempt ever made for peace will end in the greatest battle of all time—at Armageddon.

Going to Extremes

Theological extremes are generally caused by excessive reactions. A person raised in one theological context is exposed to another perspective and reacts with a total paradigm shift to the opposite view. This is especially true in matters of eschatology. For example, imagine holding to the pretribulational view without knowing why. You are challenged by a few questions to which you have no immediate answers. So you uncritically and naively switch to an opposing view.

There are many who do this; they exchange one view for another without careful study. And like a person who changes churches for no substantive reason, they can't embrace their new view without criticizing the former one in order to reinforce their choice.

Every eschatological view has some elements of truth in it, or else no one would believe it. *Pretribulationalists* believe Jesus could come at any time and want to be ready when He comes. *Mid-* and *posttribulationalists* believe we need to be prepared to suffer for our faith before He comes. *Postmillennialists* believe we must serve the king and spread His kingdom before He comes. *Amillennialists* remind us that eschatology ultimately points to heaven as our final destination.

At the same time, each eschatological view can be taken to dangerous extremes. *Pretribulational* preoccupation with the rapture has caused some to neglect developing a concern to deal with the cultural realities of our time.[16] *Mid-* and *posttribulational* concerns about deception have led some into a preoccupation with the error to neglect of a positive anticipation of the hope of Christ's coming.[17] *Postmillennial* extremes include Dominion theology and "kingdom now" claims that have led to unrealistic promises and expectations of success and prosperity.[18] Some *amillennialists* have become so focused on a heavenly spirituality that they virtually neglect earthly concerns.

The dangers are not in the views themselves, but in the extremes to which they can lead. Each eschatological view attempts to wrestle with the biblical realities of Israel, the church, the kingdom of God, the return of Christ, the judgments, and heaven and hell. In relation to these is the matter of the rapture and the questions about when, how, why, and who.

Is There Any Hope?

Nearly 2,000 years have passed since Jesus promised, "I will come again" (John 14:3). Throughout the subsequent generations of church history, believers have held tentatively to this promise. It is what the apostle Paul called "the blessed hope, and the glorious appearing of the great God and our Savior Jesus Christ" (Titus 2:13 KJV).

Behind the events of history, Christians see an enormous spiritual conflict with the powers of darkness.[19] God has clearly been at work in human history, but so has Satan. Humanity has produced its saints and sinners—its Florence Nightingales and its Adolf Hitlers. Secularists view everything as a playing out of the process of natural selection. By contrast, Christians view God as being sovereign over the natural process. Christianity begins with the presupposition that

God is at work in human history. In fact, Christianity teaches that God has already intervened in human history and will continue to do so in the future.

The secularism of the past century has left today's culture adrift in relativism, selfism, and materialism. In the meantime, postmodern culture has reached the point in its intellectual journey where it does not want to face the consequences of a secular world without God. But instead of turning to God, many people are now turning to a kind of scientific mysticism that combines transcendentalism, spiritualism, transpersonal psychology, and globalism.[20]

Humanity's need for a moral compass has led people to express concern for nature, animals, and human rights, with little interest in objective biblical truth. In such an environment, it is little wonder that the latest generations do not want to do the hard work of wrestling with objective biblical statements about the future.

In the meantime, the storm that is gathering on the horizon looks more ominous all the time. The political tensions grow deeper. Economies around the world are becoming more unstable. The social fabric of society is unraveling. The realignment of the nations on the European continent leaves many questions about the future of Europe. The resurgence of Russia and the continued conflicts in the Middle East unnerve us all, for they are a constant reminder of how quickly the march to Armageddon could begin.

As the Western world continues to move further away from its biblical roots, it is taking the same path Israel took during the days of the Judges, when everyone did what was "right in his own eyes" (Judges 21:25). Israel's downward spiral began with a series of spiritual compromises that eventually led to moral corruption and resulted in civil catastrophe. Over time, the spiritual, moral, and social fabric of Israeli society disintegrated. The closing chapters of the book of Judges (17–21) serve as an appendix to the rest of the book. They give the reader a behind-the-scenes look at what was going wrong during those days. It was a time of spiritual failure and moral confusion, which ultimately resulted in a civil war. The very people God promised to bless were on the verge of extinction.

One does not have to look far to see a similar pattern emerging in America and Europe today—indeed, in the entire civilized world. Material prosperity, accelerated by advanced technology, has propelled our world to the point of such self-reliance that many people see little need for God. Biblical concepts of truth and morality are considered out of step with the times. Al Mohler has observed that when that which was once celebrated is condemned and that which was once condemned is celebrated and those who refuse to join the celebration are marginalized, you have the death of a culture.[21]

Time to Get Serious

In view of the darkness of our times, David Jeremiah quotes the great Scottish preacher Duncan Campbell, who said, "There is a growing conviction everywhere, and especially among thoughtful people, that unless revival comes, other forces will take the field, that will sink us further into the mire of humanism and materialism."[22] Dr. Jeremiah then adds, "The good news is that revival is possible—and we have the history to prove it."[23] After tracing the history of American revivals over the past two centuries, he then calls for a revival of prayer and practice by today's believers. All this from a pretribulationalist who believes in a future rapture but has not abandoned his concern for the present world!

There have always been two opposite extremes among prophetic opinions: One extreme finds prophetic fulfillments in virtually every contemporary event, while the other extreme cynically blinds its eyes to any possible fulfillment at all. We believe the key to properly interpreting eschatology is a balance that avoids both extremes. Excessive speculation, date-setting, and date-suggesting based on complicated mathematical calculations have led to both erroneous and ridiculous conclusions that often cause people to reject the legitimate study of Bible prophecy.[24]

At the same time, avoiding the study of Bible prophecy means avoiding more than 25 percent of the biblical text. Altogether, there are more than 1,000 prophecies in the Bible, half of which have already been fulfilled.[25] These provide us with a pattern of prediction and fulfillment that can guide us as we attempt to interpret those predictions yet to be fulfilled in the future. Any legitimate study of these prophecies must begin with a study of the Scriptures themselves. In other words, let the Bible speak for itself!

The apostle Peter reminds us "that no prophecy of Scripture is a matter of one's own interpretation, for no prophecy was ever made by an act of human will, but men moved by the Holy Spirit spoke from God" (2 Peter 1:20-21). If their messages were inspired of God, we dare not fail to heed their warnings and promises.

CHAPTER 3

Raptures in the Bible

*[Rapture] describes God's activity in
physically and miraculously transporting
people from one place to another.[1]*

WILLIAM MOUNCE

The rapture of believers is an important biblical concept that appears in the Bible from Genesis to Revelation. The idea of believers being "caught up" by God is not limited to Paul's letter to the Thessalonians. There are several places throughout the Bible where people were "snatched up" from earth to heaven—providing insight regarding aspects of our future rapture.

As we will see, there are seven raptures of specific people clearly described in Scripture. These involve Enoch, Elijah, Jesus, Philip, Paul, and the two witnesses. It's possible that John was raptured as well, which would give us eight. In light of these raptures, any serious theological understanding of biblical eschatology must include the idea of believers being "caught up" into heaven. Again, we may differ on our understanding of the timing of the rapture to come, but not the reality that it will take place.

Interestingly, some critics argue there is no rapture at all for the church. Yet we will see the word we refer to as the rapture is used 14 times in the New Testament. In addition, several raptures have already taken place in Scripture or are specifically mentioned in the future. Those who claim there will be no rapture do so in contradiction to the direct teachings of Scripture.

Others agree there will be a future rapture, yet differ in regard to the timing of this event. In addition to the pretribulational view of the rapture, there are those who hold to a midtribulation,[2] prewrath,[3] and posttribulation view.[4] A minority even suggests a partial-rapture view, in which believers leave the earth at various times based on their faithfulness to Christ.[5] However, a look at the biblical references to all the raptures in the Bible reveal several interesting insights that consistently strengthen the position of the pretribulation rapture view, which states that all believers will be taken from this world prior to all the judgments to come during the tribulation period.

The Word Rapture

The word *rapture* comes from the Latin word *raptus*, meaning "to snatch up, to seize, or to carry off by force." In the Greek New Testament, this word is *harpazō*. It is used 14 times in seven books in the New Testament:

> *Matthew 11:12:* "From the days of John the Baptist until now the kingdom of heaven suffers violence, and violent men take it *by force.*"

> *Matthew 12:29:* "How can anyone enter the strong man's house and *carry off* his property, unless he first binds the strong man? And then he will plunder his house."

> *Matthew 13:19:* "When anyone hears the word of the kingdom and does not understand it, the evil one comes and *snatches away* what has been sown in his heart."

> *John 6:15:* "So Jesus, perceiving that they were intending to come and *take* Him *by force* to make Him king, withdrew again to the mountain by Himself alone."

John 10:12: "He who is a hired hand, and not a shepherd, who is not the owner of the sheep, sees the wolf coming, and leaves the sheep and flees, and the wolf *snatches* them and scatters them."

John 10:28: "I give eternal life to them, and they will never perish; and no one will *snatch* them out of My hand."

John 10:29: "My Father, who has given them to Me, is greater than all; and no one is able to *snatch* them out of the Father's hand."

Acts 8:39: "When they came up out of the water, the Spirit of the Lord *snatched* Philip *away*."

Acts 23:10: "As a great dissension was developing, the commander was afraid Paul would be torn to pieces by them and ordered the troops to go down and take him away from them *by force*, and bring him into the barracks."

2 Corinthians 12:2: "I know a man in Christ who fourteen years ago—whether in the body I do not know, or out of the body I do not know, God knows—such a man was *caught up* to the third heaven."

2 Corinthians 12:4: "…was *caught up* into Paradise and heard inexpressible words, which a man is not permitted to speak."

1 Thessalonians 4:17: "Then we who are alive and remain will be *caught up* together with them in the clouds to meet the Lord in the air, and so we shall always be with the Lord."

Jude 23: "…save others, *snatching* them out of the fire; and on some have mercy with fear, hating even the garment polluted by the flesh."

Revelation 12:5: "She gave birth to a son, a male child, who is to rule all the nations with a rod of iron; and her child was *caught up* to God and to His throne."

Of these 14 uses of *harpazō*, four refer to an actual rapture by God. In addition to believers, both dead and living (1 Thessalonians 4:17), these include Philip (Acts 8:39), Paul (2 Corinthians 2:2-3), and the male child (Revelation 12:5).[6] The other references occur in relation to earthly events, such as soldiers snatching up Paul "by force" from the crowd (Acts 23:10) or "snatching" people from a sinful way of life (Jude 1:23). Other passages in the New Testament mention a rapture event without the use of the word *harpazō*, which we will discuss later in this chapter.

Raptures in the Old Testament
In addition to references to the word translated "rapture" in the New Testament, the Old Testament reveals two occasions on which the Lord "snatched up" a person into heaven. On both occasions, the person was taken alive directly to heaven with the Lord. Thus, the idea of a miraculous rapture of God's people has a precedence in the Old Testament.

Enoch
The first record of such an event has to do with Enoch. He is an intriguing character in Scripture, mentioned six times in Genesis, once in a genealogy in 1 Chronicles 1:3, and three times in the New Testament (Luke 3:37; Hebrews 11:5; Jude 14).[7]

Enoch was the son of Jared (Genesis 5:18) and became the father of Methuselah at the age of 65, and later he had other sons and daughters (Genesis 5:21-22). Living in the time of the early patriarchs, he lived to the age of 365. Scripture then notes, "Enoch walked with God; and he was not, for God *took him*" (Genesis 5:24). John Sailhamer notes, "Enoch is an example of one who found life amid the curse of death. In Enoch the author is able to show that the pronouncement of death is not the last word that need be said about a person's life. One can find life if one 'walks with God.'"[8]

Enoch (Hebrew, *Henok*) means "beginner" or "founder."[9] A descendant of Adam, Enoch was the seventh generation from Adam in the line of Seth, even as evil Lamech was the seventh from Adam in the line of Cain. Lutheran scholar H.C. Leupold notes the fact that to say Enoch "walked with God" signifies to "walk about" or "to live" in intimacy with God, a concept mentioned only of Enoch (Genesis 5:22, 24) and Noah (Genesis 6:9).[10] He then adds, "The expression 'he was not' (*enennu*) means he was translated...It could not mean he died...because 'God *took* him' (*laqach*) involves the same word as that used in the translation of Elijah (2 Kings 2:3, 5)... Standing thus halfway between Adam and the flood, this translation of Enoch constitutes a most welcome testimony to the prospects of eternal life."[11]

Dutch Reformed scholar G.Ch. Aalders suggests, "I prefer the reading, 'God took him to Himself.' The word certainly implies that the object taken is separated from its prior environment...it is obvious that Enoch was removed from this present world and brought into the presence of God."[12] John Calvin comments, "He must be shamelessly contentious, who will not acknowledge that something extraordinary is here pointed out...Enoch was taken out of this world by an unusual mode, and was received by the Lord in a miraculous manner...[he] vanished from the sight of men, as we read was also done with respect to Elijah."[13]

In the three New Testament references to Enoch, we learn two additional facts. Jude 14 refers to Enoch proclaiming a prophecy about the Lord's coming.[14] Hebrews 11:5 also notes, "By faith Enoch was taken up so that he would not see death; and he was not found because God took him up; for he obtained the witness that before his being taken up he was pleasing to God." The final phrase, "he was pleasing to God," indicates Enoch's standing before the Lord.

His rapture foreshadows the rapture of the church, in which the Lord will take those He is pleased with (all true believers in Christ) to be with Him. Just as Enoch escaped the coming judgment that took place through the flood in the time of Noah (Genesis 6–8), believers will escape the judgment of the tribulation period through a pretribulation rapture.

Elijah

The second Old Testament person taken alive directly into heaven was the prophet Elijah. Elijah ("my God is Yahweh") was a ninth-century BC prophet from Tishbe, in Gilead, on the east bank of the northern kingdom of Israel (1 Kings 17:7).[15] Elijah's early ministry involved several confrontations with the idolatrous Ahab and Jezebel, the king and queen of Israel. This reached a climax at Mt. Carmel, where Elijah challenged the prophets of Baal to call down fire from heaven (1 Kings 18:19-39). Despite God's miraculous intervention, Jezebel determined to have Elijah killed, so he fled to the desert and hid in a cave (1 Kings 19:1-9). There, God called Elijah to anoint Elisha as his successor (19:15). Leaving the cave, he found Elisha and "threw his mantle on him" (19:19). For about the next ten years they ministered together, training "sons of the prophets" (disciples) in the various cities of Israel and Judah (2 Kings 2:3).

Second Kings 2 begins, "It came about when the LORD was about to *take up* Elijah by a whirlwind to heaven, that Elijah went with Elisha from Gilgal" (verse 1). His servant Elisha refused to leave his side, staying with Elijah as they walked to Bethel, Jericho, and across the Jordan River after Elijah parted the water by striking it with his cloak (1 Kings 2:8). Verses 11-12 report, "As they were going along and talking, behold, there appeared a chariot of fire and horses of fire which separated the two of them. And Elijah went up by a whirlwind to heaven. Elisha saw *it* and cried out, 'My father, my father, the chariots of Israel and its horsemen!' And he saw Elijah no more."

C.F. Keil and Franz Delitzsch comment, "As God did formerly take Enoch away, so that he did not taste death (Genesis 5:24), so did He also suddenly take Elijah away from Elisha, and carry him into heaven without dying."[16] As a result, Elisha picked up the fallen mantle and carried on the elder prophet's ministry (2 Kings 2:13-15). Thus, Keil concludes, "Elijah did not die, but was received into heaven by being 'changed' (1 Corinthians 15:51-52; 1 Thessalonians 4:15)."[17]

No specific explanation is provided to account for Elijah's direct ascent into heaven. However, it is clear in his case he had performed the Lord's will as a prophet in Israel and had finished his work, which was left to Elisha. While Elijah had been told to anoint Hazael as king of Syria and Jehu as king of Israel, it was, in fact, Elisha who carried out the prophet's mandate and anointed the two kings (2 Kings 8:13; 9:6). In the meantime, some of the prophet's disciples questioned whether the Spirit of the Lord had taken Elijah to some distant mountain. But Elisha assured them that even if they looked they would not find him—he was convinced Elijah had been taken to heaven (2 Kings 2:16-18).

Rather than escaping a coming judgment, it appears the focus in Elijah's example was a blessing rewarded for his service to the Lord. This, too, foreshadows one of the purposes of the yet-future pretribulation rapture. Believers will not only escape the judgment of the tribulation; they will also receive the blessing of following the Lord. However, just as men questioned the disappearance of the prophet Elijah, so they will likely question the rapture of the church.

Raptures in the New Testament

Seven raptures are recorded in the New Testament. These include the ascension of Jesus (Greek, *harpasthē* in Revelation 12:5), the temporary raptures of Philip and Paul, the calling up (Greek, *anaba*) of John, the resurrection and rapture of the two witnesses in Revelation 11:12, and the rapture of all believers in 1 Thessalonians 4:13-18.

Jesus

First, Jesus ascended to heaven following His resurrection. This event, known as the ascension, is described in Acts 1:9-11 (it is also mentioned in Luke 24:51). After 40 days of appearances (Acts 1:3), we read:

> After He had said these things, He was *lifted up* while they were looking on, and a cloud received Him out of their sight. And as they were gazing intently into the sky while He was going, behold, two men in white clothing stood beside them. They also said, "Men of Galilee, why do you stand looking into the sky? This Jesus, who has been taken up from you into heaven, will come in just the same way as you have watched Him go into heaven."

What is intriguing about this rapture of Jesus is that the angels reported Jesus will return "in just the same way" as the disciples had watched Him go into heaven. What way was this? Jesus left by being "lifted up" (Greek, *epērthē*) and "received" (Greek, *hupelaben*) by a cloud. His ascension was physical, personal, visible, and glorious. Jesus promised to one day return in the same way at the second coming (Matthew 24:30; see Daniel 7:13) as well as to the same place, the Mount of Olives (Zechariah 14:4). John Maile summarizes the significance of the ascension narratives in Luke and Acts as follows:

1. The ascension is the confirmation of the exaltation of Christ and his present lordship.

2. It is the explanation of the continuity between the ministry of Jews and that of the church.

3. It is the culmination of the resurrection appearances.

4. It is the prelude to the sending of the Spirit.

5. It is the foundation of Christian mission.

6. It is the pledge of the return of Christ.[18]

F.F. Bruce notes the parallel references to "clouds" in the biblical passages regarding the transfiguration (Matthew 17:5; Mark 9:26; Luke 9:34), the ascension (Acts 1:9), and the *parousia* (Mark 13:26; Matthew 24:30; Luke 21:27) as "three successive manifestations of Christ's divine glory."[19] Darrell Bock follows Bruce, noting that Christ's resurrection/exaltation/ascension are "one continuous movement" that points to His ultimate exaltation in glory.[20]

The ascension of Christ is also depicted symbolically in Revelation 12:5 as the male (child)—who will rule all nations—being "caught up" (Greek, *harpasthe*) to God and His throne. It is clear in this context that the reference is to Jesus's ascension into heaven. The fact that the Apocalypse uses the same word to speak of the ascension as 1 Thessalonians 4:17 uses to speak of the rapture (Greek, *harpagsometha*) clearly indicates Jesus's ascension is a form of rapture.

J. Dwight Pentecost notes, "Having completed all that the Father had given Him to do, the Lord Jesus Christ 'was taken up to glory' (1 Timothy 3:16) where 'he sat down at the right hand of the Majesty in heaven' (Hebrews 1:3)."[21] Christ, having promised to return to this world, will then "sit on His glorious throne" (Matthew 25:31). Thus, the ascension of Christ to heaven at the beginning of the church age will be followed by the rapture of His bride (1 Thessalonians 4:16-17) and their marriage in heaven (Revelation 19:11-16).

Philip

The second rapture noted in the New Testament is also recorded in the book of Acts (8:25-40). In this passage, Philip is led by an angel to meet with an Ethiopian eunuch. A Hellenistic Jew, Philip was one of the seven original deacons appointed by the church in Jerusalem (Acts 6:1-7). After Philip successfully evangelized Samaria

(Acts 8:1-8), he was led by an angel to head south toward Gaza, on the edge of the Sinai desert. Darrell Bock calls this region the "last water stop in southwestern Israel before entering the desert on the way to Egypt."[22]

There, Philip encountered an Ethiopian of African descent who was reading from the scroll of the prophet Isaiah. Eunuchs often served as court officials (see Ebed-melech in Jeremiah 38:7-13). As a Gentile eunuch, he would have been restricted to serving in the court of the Gentiles and not allowed full participation in Jewish worship, even if he were a proselyte (see Deuteronomy 23:1). Philip shared the good news of Jesus with the eunuch, speaking from Isaiah 53 in response to the eunuch's question, "Of whom does the prophet say this?" (Acts 8:34). "As they went along the road they came to some water; and the eunuch said, 'Look! Water! What prevents me from being baptized?'" (Acts 8:36).

This powerful account then chronicles Philip baptizing the first known convert from Ethiopia. Walter Elwell observes, "Philip, by his eager preaching of Christ, first to the Samaritans and then to the Ethiopian, reflected the way the gospel penetrated social barriers and dissolved racial prejudices and demonstrated that the grace of God in Christ Jesus is freely available to all."[23]

The eunuch's baptism was not the end of God's power in this account. After the baptism, Philip's rapture occurs: "When they came up out of the water, the Spirit of the Lord *snatched* Philip away; and the eunuch no longer saw him, but went on his way rejoicing. But Philip found himself at Azotus, and as he passed through he kept preaching the gospel to all the cities until he came to Caesarea" (Acts 8:39-40).

The verb translated "baptize" (Greek, *baptizō*) is used 21 times in Acts in fulfillment of Matthew 28:19-20 and Acts 2:38. Bock notes, "The verb here for being caught up (*harpazō*) appears twice in Acts...and twelve other times in the NT...his instant removal makes clearer still that God is at work. It recalls Jesus's removal in

Luke 24:31."[24] John R.W. Stott observes, in this case, Philip was "removed with miraculous velocity…as at the rapture."[25] He was "snatched away" and reappeared at Azotus (Ashdod) some 20 miles away. Stott adds that the eunuch went on his way "without the evangelist but with the evangel, without human aid but with the divine Spirit."[26] In the meantime, Philip continued preaching the gospel on the Mediterranean coast until he reached Caesarea (verse 40), some 60 miles to the north, where he eventually made his home (Acts 21:8). The entire account (Acts 8:25-40) indicates God's supernatural activity in the instantaneous removal of Philip from the eunuch's presence.

There are two significant observations to be made with regard to Philip's rapture. First, it took place by the Spirit of the Lord, the Holy Spirit. This is the first mention of the third Person of the Trinity being involved in a rapture event. Certainly Father, Son, and Spirit will be involved in the future rapture of all believers. Second, the passage notes that after the baptism, "the eunuch no longer saw" Philip. Though Philip was only temporarily raptured to another location, this event highlights an important aspect of the future rapture of the church: Those who remain on the earth will no longer see those who were raptured.

Paul

The third rapture recorded in the New Testament involves the apostle Paul. In 2 Corinthians 12, Paul refers to "a man" who was caught up into heaven. Though he does not directly identify himself in this passage, from the context it is clear that he is speaking of himself. In verses 1-4 we read this:

> Boasting is necessary, though it is not profitable; but I will go on to visions and revelations of the Lord. I know a man in Christ who fourteen years ago—whether in the body I do not know, or out of the body I do not

know, God knows—such a man was *caught up* to the
third heaven. And I know how such a man—whether
in the body or apart from the body I do not know, God
knows—was *caught up* into Paradise and heard inexpressible words, which a man is not permitted to speak.

The Norwegian theologian Olaf Moe said, "Paul is not only the
greatest missionary of the Christian church; he is also the greatest teacher...by virtue of his peculiar qualifications and his unique
gifts, he has erected a structure of doctrine that has become the
main foundation of all later Christian theology, especially among
the evangelical faiths."[27] Scottish scholar F.F. Bruce wrote, "Paul's
letters are our primary source for his life and work, a primary source
for our knowledge of the beginnings of Christianity, for they are
the earliest datable Christian documents."[28] From these letters and
biographical accounts in the book of Acts we correlate the events of
Paul's life. His missionary endeavors took him from Israel to Rome
within a span of less than twenty years.

It has long been observed that 2 Corinthians is Paul's most personal and passionate letter. In none of Paul's other letters do we find
so much autobiographical information related to persons, events,
problems, and situations in the apostle's life and ministry, It is, in
fact, these specific details that shout to us of the authenticity of this
letter, including Paul's account of being raptured into heaven.

Most scholars agree 2 Corinthians was written about AD 56–57.
This rapture would have occurred 14 years earlier, or about AD
42–44—a decade after the resurrection of Jesus. Though reluctant
to speak about his experience, Paul notes several details referring to
his being "caught up" to the "third heaven" (the third heaven refers
to the place where God lives—beyond the first heaven, or the sky,
and the second heaven, or outer space).

Paul speaks of himself in the third person to describe his "rapture of ineffable exaltation" prior to sharing about his experience

with the thorn in the flesh (verse 7). Anglican scholar Philip Edge-
cumbe Hughes comments, "Indeed, the concept of bodily rapture
formed an important element in his eschatological teaching."[29] After
Paul opens his heart to his readers, he shares about the experience
he had 14 years earlier, and admits he was not sure whether he was
"in the body" or "out of the body" (verse 2). What he did know was
that he was "caught up" (*harpazō*) into the third heaven either physically or spiritually. Dan Mitchell notes that Paul had already used
the term *harpazō* to describe the rapture of living believers in 1 Thessalonians 4:17 (written in AD 51). Mitchell suggests, "Inasmuch as
he has already used this term to speak of the common experience
of believers occurring at the coming of Christ for his saints, it is not
inappropriate to speculate if Paul came at this time to understand
this 'mystery' as he calls it in 1 Corinthians 15:51."[30]

First, Paul was raptured "into Paradise." It was common to speak
of heaven as "Paradise" (Luke 23:43; Revelation 2:7). Therefore
Mitchell adds, "Thus, whether the 'third heaven' (v. 2) was viewed
on the way to heaven or synonymous with it, Paul's celestial journey eventually took him to heaven."[31] He was in the presence of
the Lord immediately following his rapture. In a similar way, 1 Corinthians 15:52 reveals the rapture of believers will take place "in a
moment, in the twinkling of the eye." Some refer to the speed of
this event as creating a "secret rapture," a snatching up that takes
place so quickly that no one will see it occur. However, it will be no
secret that it did occur. Millions of people will disappear from earth
in an instant, leaving the ungodly of the world in havoc as they seek
to understand what has just happened. This event will be anything
but a secret!

Second, this rapture occurred to "a man in Christ." John Drane
sees this concept as the heart of Paul's theology. He writes, "The
supreme fact for Paul was that he was 'a man in Christ.' It was by
being 'in Christ' that a person could be justified before God, and
share in the new life Jesus had come to bring."[32] Another distinction

of all raptures recorded in Scripture is that they occur to God's people. Such information should urge believers to faithfully share the gospel with everyone possible, knowing the time is short and that not everyone will be taken in the rapture. In fact, only those "in Christ" will be taken, according to 1 Thessalonians 4:14, 16.

Third, Paul "heard inexpressible words." One of the beautiful aspects believers can anticipate about being in the presence of Christ is the supernatural fellowship that will occur from being with the Lord. Paul could not even speak of what took place during his experience. Imagine how much greater of an experience it will be when we live in Christ's presence forever! This brings up an important point: Bible prophecies about the future are not intended to scare believers; they are intended to prepare us for the great and inexpressible glory that will be ours when Jesus comes to take us to the Father's house (John 14:1-3).

John

The fourth possible rapture recorded in the New Testament is found in Revelation. Due to anti-Christian persecution that took place under the Roman emperor Domitian, the apostle John was banished to the island of Patmos. While there, he continued to worship the Lord and wrote the book of Revelation. He states in Revelation 1:9-11, that he was on the island of Patmos because of "the testimony of Jesus." Then he adds, "I was in the Spirit on the Lord's day, and I heard behind me a loud voice like the sound of a trumpet, saying, 'Write in a book what you see, and send it to the seven churches: to Ephesus and to Smyrna and to Pergamum and to Thyatira and to Sardis and to Philadelphia and to Laodicea.'"

In Revelation 4:1-2, John refers back to this vision and says, "After these things I looked, and behold, a door standing open in heaven, and the first voice which I had heard, like the sound of a trumpet speaking with me, said, '*Come up* here, and I will show you what must take place after these things.' Immediately I was in the

Spirit; and behold, a throne was standing in heaven, and One sitting on the throne."

John Walvoord observes that while the invitation to John to "come up here" (Greek, *anaba hōde*) is similar to that which the church anticipates at the rapture, "it is clear from the context that this is not an explicit reference to the rapture of the church, as John was not actually translated; in fact he was still in his natural body on the island of Patmos."[33] However, there is no clear reference to where his body actually was located. Whether "in the body" or "out of the body," as in the case of Paul (2 Corinthians 12:1-3), John was, in Walvoord's words, temporarily "translated into scenes of heaven."[34] Robert Thomas views chapter 4 as a new "vision of the court of heaven." As such, Thomas calls it a summons to "assume a new vantage point for the sake of the revelation he was about to receive."[35]

While John's experience involved being called up to heaven, it is impossible to determine from the text whether he was actually raptured there, for the word *harpazō* is not used to describe this event. Nevertheless, the idea of his being transported, even in a vision, shows a pattern of a believer being taken to heaven to gain a new perspective on events that would transpire on earth. The fact that John saw the white robed "elders" in heaven wearing golden crowns most likely indicates that they represent the raptured believers in heaven prior to the tribulation, which follows in chapters 6–19.[36]

Future Raptures

In addition to the raptures that have already taken place throughout Scripture, two future raptures are noted.

The Rapture of Living Believers

The entire focus of this book is on the pretribulation view of the rapture of all believers in Christ. While there are several passages that describe the rapture, the three most direct passages include John 14:1-3, 1 Corinthians 15:51-58, and 1 Thessalonians 4:13-18.

In John 14:1-3, Jesus personally describes some aspects of the rapture. First, He explains that one reason for leaving earth is so He can personally prepare a place for us in heaven. This amazing detail reveals Jesus is actively involved in preparing our future heavenly home!

Second, in John 14:3 Jesus teaches, "If I go and prepare a place for you, I will come again and *receive you* to Myself, that where I am, there you may be also." The order of events is clear. Jesus will leave (the ascension), He will prepare a place for us in heaven, He will come again, He will take us to be with Him (the rapture), and we will be in heaven with Him. This order closely parallels the details of 1 Corinthians 15:51-58 and 1 Thessalonians 4:13-18 in ways other views of the rapture do not.

In 1 Corinthians 15:51-58, the order is as follows:

1. Living believers transformed: "we will not all sleep, but we will all be changed."

2. This transformation will take place in a single moment: "in the twinkling of an eye."

3. A trumpet will sound: "the trumpet will sound."

4. Dead believers will be raised: "the dead will be raised imperishable."

5. Believers will be changed (both the dead in Christ and those still alive on earth): "we will be changed."

Interestingly, the passage concludes with encouragement for believers: "Therefore, my beloved brethren, be steadfast, immovable, always abounding in the work of the Lord, knowing that your toil is not in vain in the Lord" (1 Corinthians 15:58). The rapture is repeatedly noted as a source of encouragement for living believers. It will include the resurrection of the dead in Christ, the rapture of living believers, and being reunited with all believers together with the Lord. Thus, it involves a resurrection, a rapture, and a return.

First Thessalonians 4:13-18 offers additional details regarding the rapture, and includes this encouragement, "We do not want you to be uninformed, brethren, about those who are asleep, so that you will not grieve as do the rest who have no hope" (verse 13). Similar to the passage in 1 Corinthians 15, the order notes the transformation of believers, with the dead in Christ raised first, followed by living believers "caught up" (Greek, *harpagēsometha*) with the Lord, uniting all believers together in the presence of the Lord forever. Paul concludes once again with encouragement, saying, "Therefore comfort one another with these words" (verse 18).

The Rapture of the Two Witnesses

In Revelation 11:3-12 we read about the rapture of the two witnesses sent by God to testify to the world on His behalf. God will grant these two Jewish men authority to witness and prophesy for 42 months, or 1,260 days—this comprises the first three-and-a-half years of the seven-year tribulation that will follow the rapture (verses 2-3). These two men will minister outside of the rebuilt Jerusalem temple and have the ability to destroy their enemies (verse 5). Like Elijah, they will be able to stop rain from falling. Like Moses, they will be able to turn water into blood and strike the earth with plagues (verse 6).

At the midpoint of the tribulation, the beast (antichrist) will kill the two witnesses and leave their dead bodies in the streets of Jerusalem for three-and-a-half days (verses 7-8). The people of the world will celebrate their death (verse 10). Yet these two witnesses will return to life after three-and-a-half days, causing great fear among the people (verse 11). They will then follow the Lord's command to "come up here," and they will be raptured to heaven (verse 12). After that, a great earthquake will destroy one-tenth of Jerusalem, killing 7,000 people and causing those who remain to glorify God (verse 13).

While the term *harpazō* is not used to describe the rapture of the two "witnesses" (Greek, *martusin*), also called "prophets" (Greek, *prophētai*), the fact of their physical resurrection and rapture is clearly indicated. A voice from heaven called them to "come up here" (Greek, *anabate hōde*) and they "went up" (Greek, *anebēsan*) (verse 12). The initial call is the same as that given to John in Revelation 4:1. But whereas John was "in the Spirit" (4:2), the witnesses are described as literally going up into heaven in resurrected bodies just as those "in Christ" will be resurrected and raptured up to heaven (see 1 Thessalonians 4:13-18).

Though some interpret the rapture of the two witnesses as a symbolic act, the text provides a straightforward reading regarding their ministry in the last days. In Scripture's account of this future rapture, three important points emerge: First, the two witnesses will ascend into heaven at the time the Lord says, "Come." Second, their enemies will remain on earth. And third, judgment will follow. This pattern supports the chronology presented in the pretribulational rapture view.

We might ask, "Why would God raise up these two witnesses to preach in Jerusalem during the tribulation to allow them to be killed, and then resurrect them and rapture them to heaven?" If in fact the greater rapture of the church has already taken place (1 Thessalonians 4:13-18), this mini-rapture of the two witnesses will serve as a testimony to the tribulation saints that the greater rapture was indeed a supernatural and miraculous intervention carried out by God.

The Rapture of the Male Child

One final rapture is noted in Revelation 12:5: "She gave birth to a son, a male child, who is to rule all the nations with a rod of iron; and her child was *caught up* to God and to His throne." The language in this chapter is clearly visionary. It is the telling of "a great sign…in heaven" (Revelation 12:1). The players in this eschatological drama involve a woman, a red dragon, a male child, and the angel Michael. The identity of the individuals in this vision are as follows:

- The woman: Israel
- The red dragon: Satan
- The male child: Jesus
- Michael: archangel

Though there is some debate about the identity of the woman in Revelation 12:1-2, certain contextual clues clearly identify her as Israel. The passage speaks of a crown, the sun, the moon, and the stars, all of which are closely connected with Old Testament references to Israel (Genesis 37:9-11; Isaiah 26:17-18; 66:7-9; Jeremiah 4:31).[37]

The dragon is self-identified in the text as Satan. He and his angels will wage war with the archangel Michael in heaven. Revelation 12:9 tells us the outcome of this battle: "The great dragon was thrown down, the serpent of old who is called the devil and Satan, who deceives the whole world; he was thrown down to the earth, and his angels were thrown down with him."

The male child is one "who is to rule all the nations with a rod of iron; and [he will be] caught up to God and to His throne" (verse 5). Who is the one who will rule the nations and be with God in heaven? The clear answer is Jesus Christ. He is the child who came into the world, was pursued by Satan, and will show Himself victorious.

According to verse 5, this child is to be "caught up" (Greek, *harpasthē*) to God. Erich Tiedtke comments, "In Rev 12:5 the child (Jesus) is caught up to God to escape the persecution of the dragon."[38] This is most certainly a reference to the ascension of Jesus Christ, which we've already reviewed in Luke 24:51 and Acts 1:9-11. Though this is mentioned in a futuristic vision, it refers to the time that includes the ascension of Jesus as an important aspect of His victory over Satan. It also clearly defines the male child as Jesus.

The Blessed Hope

A careful study of the Greek term *harpazō* and these examples of biblical raptures make it clear that the idea of a future rapture of all believers is certainly biblical. The only real debate is over the matter of the *timing* of the rapture, not the *fact* that there will be such an event. Therefore, any serious discussion about the nature, timing, and significance of the rapture ought to be carried out with the utmost respect for this biblical concept. If the first Christians viewed the rapture as "the blessed hope" (Titus 2:13), then so should we, regardless of our opinions with regard to its timing.

Raptures in the Bible	
Person(s)	*Reference*
Enoch	Genesis 5:24
Elijah	2 Kings 2:11-12
Jesus's ascension	Revelation 12:5
Philip (temporary)	Acts 8:39-40
Paul (temporary)	2 Corinthians 12:1-4
John (possibly)	Revelation 4:1-2
Living believers	1 Thessalonians 4:13-18
Two witnesses	Revelation 11:11-12

CHAPTER 4

Rapture Views—It's About Time

*True Christians will be taken out of danger
before God's wrath is poured out on the
earth...The unsaved will be left.*[1]

FRANCIS SCHAEFFER

So far, we've established that the rapture or catching away of living believers to heaven is a biblical doctrine. Scripture clearly teaches that at some point in the future, Jesus will come, and every believer in Christ who is alive on earth will be caught up to heaven to meet Him in the air. The issue isn't *will* there be a rapture, but *when* will it happen in relation to other end-time events. The pivotal question is this: Will the church of Jesus Christ go through none, some portion, or all of the seven-year tribulation before the rapture occurs?

The timing of the rapture is one of the most controversial and hotly debated issues in eschatology. In January 2016, 1,000 Protestant pastors and ministers were surveyed and asked the following question: Which one of the following statements best describes your views on when the biblical rapture will occur? These were the options:

- The rapture has already occurred (a view associated with preterism)

- Christians will be taken up before the tribulation period that precedes the second coming (often called the pretribulation view)

- Christians will be taken up in the middle of the tribulation period that precedes the second coming (often called the midtribulation view)

- Christians will be taken up before the great wrath of God is poured out late in the tribulation period that precedes the second coming (often called the prewrath view)

- The rapture and the second coming are describing events that will unfold simultaneously or close together at the end of the tribulation (often called the postribulation view)

- The concept of the rapture is not to be taken literally

- None of these

- Not sure

Here are the results of the survey:

> Overall, 36 percent of pastors—the largest proportion by far—aligned themselves with the pretribulation view, with the second largest proportion (25 percent) saying that "the concept of the rapture is not to be taken literally." An additional 18 percent aligned themselves with the posttribulation belief that the rapture and the second coming of Christ are essentially one and the same.[2]

According to this survey, the pretrib position is the dominant view, but it continues to come under withering fire, especially from postrib proponents. The pretrib view is denied and often despised by many, while a growing number of professing Christians see the whole issue as irrelevant. More and more believers today appear to be agnostic about issues related to the end times, especially the timing of the rapture. Renald Showers observes,

> When confronted with the issue of when the Rapture of the church will take place, many Christians respond, "Pretrib, midtrib, postrib! So what? What difference does it make?" Others exclaim, "If it doesn't affect my salvation, I couldn't care less about when it happens!" Still others try to dodge the issue by stating either, "I'm pro-Rapturist—I'm for it!" or "I'm a pan-Rapturist—I believe it will all pan out."
>
> Does it really matter when Christ will come to take His bride to be with Him? Should the timing of the Rapture make any practical difference in the life of a Christian, or is the issue so insignificant that Christians shouldn't bother with it?[3]

The timing of the rapture is a very practical matter because only the pretrib view teaches that Christ could come back at any moment. All the other rapture views require at least part or all of the tribulation to unfold before Christ can come to rapture the church. The at-any-moment possibility of Christ's coming to take us with Him to heaven should provide a sense of urgency to our service and make a difference in our "values, actions, priorities and goals."[4] Believing Jesus could come at any time should fill us with hope and expectancy and exert a purifying influence on our lives (1 John 2:2-3).

Another reason the timing of the rapture is significant is that the future of everyone reading these words will differ greatly depending on which view of the rapture's timing is correct. There's a great deal at stake with regard to which view is ultimately true. For example, if the end times begin during your lifetime, will you be on earth during the tribulation and watch the rise of the antichrist and maybe even find yourself under his brutal reign? Will you be faced with the decision to accept or reject the mark of the beast on your right hand or forehead? Will you witness the bloodbath of the Great Tribulation, when the world is plunged into the events described in Revelation 6–18? Or will you be with Christ and His people in heaven, experiencing rest, fellowship, and spiritual intimacy? Will you be here for none, half, three-fourths, or all of the tribulation? Considering the issue from this viewpoint, the timing of the rapture is a more significant issue than many people realize. It's not a minor, inconsequential theological debate.

The Timing of the Rapture

In the rest of this chapter we'll look at the five most common views regarding the timing of the rapture. We'll touch on the pretrib view only momentarily because we'll examine it more in-depth later on. And we'll spend most of our time on the other four views here, and examine their weaknesses.

Pretribulation Rapture View

Pretribulationism teaches that the rapture of the church will occur before the commencement of the seven-year tribulation period, also known as the seventieth week of Daniel. The church will not be on earth during any part of the outpouring of God's wrath. At some point after the rapture, the antichrist enters into a seven-year treaty or covenant with Israel (Daniel 9:27)—and that will mark the beginning point of the tribulation. This position was popularized in *The Scofield Reference Bible* by C.I. Scofield, *The Late Great Planet Earth* by Hal Lindsey, and the Left Behind series by Tim LaHaye and Jerry Jenkins.

The pretrib rapture is often called the "secret rapture" as a pejorative by those who disagree with it. Eckhard Schnabel describes the pretrib rapture as "the view that in the last days all true believers will be taken up to heaven in a secret rapture, leaving behind a world in chaos."[5] He later describes it as "a secret coming (to gather believers in a secret rapture)" and "a secret rapture in which the believers will disappear from the earth, leaving unbelievers behind."[6] However, we are not aware of anyone who holds to the pretrib view who considers the rapture a secret event. When Jesus comes for His people and millions all over the world disappear, the world will be shocked. The rapture will be anything but secret! Moreover, it won't be any more secret than any of the other views. The pretrib rapture should not be referred to as the secret rapture.

Midtribulation Rapture View

The midtribulation view is, in some ways, a compromise between the pretrib and posttrib views. Those who are dissatisfied with these two main options come down in the middle (literally).

Midtribulationists agree with pretribulationists "that the Rapture and Second Coming are two distinct events separated by a period of time."[7] Midtribulational rapture theory maintains that Christ will rapture His church at the midpoint of the seven-year tribulation prior to the outpouring of God's wrath. Believers will endure the first half of the seven-year tribulation, but will be exempt from the Great Tribulation, or the last half. They will be raptured before the last half of Daniel's seventieth week begins. Some noteworthy midtrib proponents are Gleason Archer, Norman B. Harrison, James Oliver Buswell, and Harold J. Ockenga.

This view makes a distinction between distress or tribulation, which has always been the lot of God's people, and the wrath of God. Believers will be caught up to heaven before the time of wrath begins at the midpoint of the seven years. The final three-and-a-half years are called the Great Tribulation.

Defending this view, Gleason Archer notes,

> It simply regards the first three and a half years, during which the Antichrist will increase his power and mount his

persecution against the church, as a lesser tribulation, not nearly as terrifying or destructive of life as those fearsome plagues that will dominate the last three and a half years. In other words, this interpretation makes a clear division between the first half as the period of the wrath of man, and the second half as the period of the wrath of God.[8]

Midtribulationists defend their view by noting the emphasis in Daniel and Revelation on the last half of the tribulation, which is variously stated as 42 months, 1,260 days, or "time, times and half a time" (Daniel 7:25; 9:27; 12:7; Revelation 11:2; 12:6, 14; 13:5). Some who hold to the midtrib view consider themselves to be the *real* pretribulationists because they believe the wrath of God and the Great Tribulation don't really begin until the midpoint of the seven years.

Midtrib advocates identify two main events in the book of Revelation as reference points for the rapture. First, J. Oliver Buswell identifies the midtrib rapture with the seventh trumpet in Revelation 11:15-19.[9] He correlates the seventh trumpet in Revelation 11 with the last trumpet in 1 Corinthians 15:52.

However, there are several prominent differences between the trumpets in 1 Corinthians 15:52 and Revelation 11:15 that indicate they should not be linked with one another.

	Trumpet in 1 Cor 15:52	Trumpet in Rev 11:15
Subject	Church	Wicked world
Result	Catching up of the church to be with the Lord	Judgment of sinners
Character	Trumpet of God's grace	Trumpet of God's judgment
Timing	Signals the close of the life of the church on earth; it's the last trumpet of the church age	Marks a climax in the progression of tribulation judgments

Just because the trumpet in 1 Corinthians 15 is called the "last" trumpet does not mean that it is the last trumpet in God's whole prophetic program. All of us who've attended school know that during the day there are several "last" bells that ring. The last bell for the nine o'clock class rings, but it's not the last bell of the day. The last bell of the lunch hour signals its end, but there are still more bells to sound.[10] Likewise, the "last" trumpet in 1 Corinthians 15:52 is the last trumpet of the church age that summons God's people to meet Jesus in the air.

Furthermore, the seventh trumpet in Revelation 11 is not the last trumpet of the end times. In Matthew 24:31 we read of a trumpet that will blast to gather the elect at the second coming of Jesus. This is three-and-a-half years after the trumpet in Revelation 11 and does not fit the chronology proposed by the midtribulation rapture view.

While most who hold to the midtrib view place the rapture at the seventh trumpet, Gleason Archer believes the harvest in Revelation 14:14-16 describes the rapture.[11]

> I looked, and behold, a white cloud, and sitting on the cloud was one like a son of man, having a golden crown on His head and a sharp sickle in His hand. And another angel came out of the temple, crying out with a loud voice to Him who sat on the cloud, "Put in your sickle and reap, for the hour to reap has come, because the harvest of the earth is ripe." Then He who sat on the cloud swung His sickle over the earth, and the earth was reaped.

The major problem with this identification is that there is no specific mention of a rapture or a resurrection in these verses; it has to be implied. Also, the surrounding context and prevailing tone of these verses is judgment, not salvation.[12]

As you can see, one of the key problems with this view is that midtribulationists can't even agree among themselves about where to place the rapture in the book of Revelation. The lack of consistency is a major weakness for this view. The reason for this lack of uniformity is "the absence of direct biblical evidence for the rapture occurring in the middle of this period."[13]

Three other serious weaknesses beset the midtrib view. First, the limiting of God's wrath to the second half of the tribulation seems doubtful in light of the six seals judgments, which take place during the first half and are specifically referred to as "the wrath of the Lamb" (Revelation 6:16-17).

Second, holding to the midtrib position means you must deny the doctrine of imminency, which asserts that Christ could return at any time. If Christ can't come until the midpoint of the tribulation, and the tribulation has not begun yet, then He can't come for at least another three-and-a-half years.

Posttribulation Rapture

Posttribulationism is the most popular view after the pretrib position. This view holds that the rapture will occur at the end of the tribulation, right before the second coming of Christ back to earth. Believers will be raptured up to meet Christ in the air and then will return immediately with Him back to the earth. Some have called this the yo-yo version of the rapture—caught up, and then returning back down immediately.

In this view, the rapture and second coming are basically viewed as one event separated by a few moments. Some posttribulationists argue that while church-age believers will be present on earth during the tribulation, God will protect them from the outpouring of His wrath. Others hold that the wrath of God will be limited to the time near the very end of the tribulation, and that God will protect believers through that time.

There are many arguments given in support of the posttribulational view. Popular pastor and author John Piper provides nine lines of argumentation to support the posttribulation view.[14] Because these arguments represent a culmination of common posttribulation works that attempt to reconcile the passages regarding Christ's future coming, let's look at them, as well as the pretribulational response to them.

First, Piper argues the word for "meeting" the Lord in the air used in 1 Thessalonians 4:17 is used in Matthew 25:6 and Acts 28:15 to refer to people going out to meet a dignitary and then accompanying him to the place from which they came out. He argues that the return of Jesus will take place in a similar manner, with believers "meeting" the Lord in the air and then returning with Him in judgment upon the earth at Armageddon. Though his argument is valid, his conclusion is not the only option. In fact, his point could support either a pretribulation or posttribulation view. The only difference in the pretribulation view is the *amount of time* between the rapture of believers to meet the Lord in the air and when they will return with Him to earth in judgment at Armageddon.

The second argument focuses on 2 Thessalonians 1:5-7. Piper suggests Paul expects to rest from his suffering at the same time and the same event as when unbelievers receive punishment, referring to Christ's coming in Revelation 19. However, Paul's words in this passage speak of the ultimate future of God's people only in general terms. Yes, God's people (the believers referred to by Paul in Thessalonica) will enter God's kingdom, and those who afflict them will receive judgment. Yet the passage does not indicate the specific *time* either of these events will occur. As is the case with 1 Thessalonians 4:17, this passage can be used to support either a pretribulation or posttribulation view.

Piper's third argument is based on 2 Thessalonians 2:1-2, in which he notes "assembling to meet him" and "the day of the Lord" refer to the same event. However, 2 Thessalonians 2:1 address two issues: (1) "the coming of our Lord Jesus Christ," and (2) "our gathering together to Him." Paul said he did not want them concerned about a message saying "that the day of the Lord has come" (2:2). Paul clearly goes on to state the antichrist will appear and the tribulation will take place before the "coming" of Jesus, or what those who hold to a pretribulation view refer to as the second coming (2:3-12). He had already addressed this aspect of the future rapture in his previous letter, noting these details in 1 Thessalonians 4:13-18. Though closely related, the rapture and second coming are not equated as the same event in this chapter.

In his fourth argument, John Piper asks this, "If Paul were a pretribulationist why did he not simply say so in 2 Thessalonians 2:3 that the Christians don't need to worry that the day of the Lord is here because all the Christians are still here? Instead he talks just the way you would expect a post-tribulational person to do."[15] As with the previous argument, this assumes "assembling to meet him" and "the day of the Lord" in 2 Thessalonians 2:1-2 refer to the same event. If they do not, and there are arguments that can be shown in favor of them being two separate events, then this question works in favor of either view.

His fifth argument focuses on the events mentioned in Matthew 24, Mark 13, and Luke 21. Piper suggests a "normal reading" gives no weight to the idea of the rapture prior to these events. This agrees with the others who hold a posttribulation view. Robert Gundry, for example, notes, "Posttribulationists equate the rapture with the gathering of the elect by angels at the sound of the trumpet (Matt. 24:31)."[16] Ultimately, this is an argument from silence. The fact there is no mention of the rapture in these passages does not determine whether the rapture does or does not take place before these events. The full counsel of Scripture must be investigated to determine the most likely interpretation.

Sixth, Piper argues, "Going through tribulation, even when it is appointed by God, is not contrary to Biblical teaching."[17] This is a true statement. The argument is not whether Christians will suffer persecution, but rather whether current believers will escape the wrath of God through a pretribulation rapture.

Seventh, Piper suggests the Bible's commands to "watch" do not lose meaning if the second coming is not an at-any-moment event. It is true that Christians are to be watchful at all times, whether one takes a pretribulational or posttribulational view of the rapture. However, those who hold to a pretribulation view suggest it is the only view that fully accounts for an imminent, at-any-moment return of Jesus, because a rapture at the *end* of the tribulation would hardly be imminent.

Eighth, Piper argues that Revelation 3:10 is open to other interpretations. This argument could be used of any passage for which multiple interpretations are possible. Even when this verse is excluded, the primary pretribulation rapture passages provide compelling evidence of an imminent rapture that remains distinct and unique from the second coming (John 14:1-3; 1 Corinthians 15:51-58; 1 Thessalonians 4:13-18).

Finally, Piper argues, "The second coming does not lose its moral power in post-tribulationism."[18] While some who hold to the pretibulation view may disagree, the pretribulation view does not exclude acceptance of this argument. Both the pretribulation rapture and the second coming should provide adequate impetus for believers on earth to live holy lives prior to each of those events.

Overall, Piper's nine arguments provide helpful nuances to the overall debate between the pretribulation and posttribulation rapture views. However, they do not result in a clear refutation of the pretribulation view, nor do they provide a thorough affirmation of the posttribulation view.

One other argument that is often cited is the connection between the "trumpet" in 1 Thessalonians 4:16 and the "last trumpet" in 1 Corinthians 15:52 with the trumpet in Matthew 24:31 at the end of the tribulation. In Matthew 24:31 we read, "He will send forth His angels with a great trumpet and they will gather together His elect from the four winds, from one end of the sky to another." Because the trumpet in Matthew 24 is sounded at the end of the tribulation and is therefore the last trumpet, posttribulation-ists believe it must be the same as the last trumpet in 1 Corinthians 15:52. However, the only similarity between these trumpets is that both are sounded to gather the Lord's people. As the following comparison reveals, the differences are significant:

	Trumpet in 1 Thess. 4:16 and 1 Cor. 15:52	Trumpet in Matt. 24:31
Subject	Church	Jewish believers in the Great Tribulation
Circumstances	Focus is on raising of believers who have died and rapturing living believers	Resurrection not mentioned; focus is on regathering living believers who have been scattered over the earth
Result	Uniting of the resurrected dead with the living in a great meeting with the Lord in the air	The elect are living believers who are regathered from all over the earth to meet the Lord, who has returned to the earth in visible glory
Signs	Preceded by no signs	Preceded by many signs (Matthew 24:4-30)

A major difficulty with the posttrib position becomes evident upon reading Matthew 25:31-33, which describes Jesus's judgment of the people still alive on earth at the time of His second coming.

> When the Son of Man comes in His glory, and all the angels with Him, then He will sit on His glorious throne. All the nations will be gathered before Him; and He will separate them from one another, as the shepherd separates the sheep from the goats; and He will put the sheep on His right, and the goats on the left.

In this assembly of people, believers are pictured as sheep, while unbelievers are depicted as goats. The problem for the postrib view is that if the rapture occurs as Jesus is descending to earth at His second coming, as posttrib proponents believe, that means all the sheep will caught up to meet Him in the air, leaving no sheep on earth for this judgment. Only goats will be left. No further separation will be necessary. Charles Ryrie underscores the problem this raises for the posttrib position:

> If the rapture occurs at the end of the Tribulation—that is, at the second coming—and if all the sheep are taken to heaven in that rapture, how will there be any left to be assembled before Christ when He comes? They will already have gone. To put it another way: The rapture/ second coming will separate the redeemed from the wicked; yet this judgment at the second coming will do the same, only there will not be any righteous on the earth to separate, since they will just have been raptured.[19]

This passage poses an insurmountable problem for the posttrib view.

Another convincing argument against the posttrib view is the absence of any reference to the rapture in Revelation 19:11-21, which is the classic New Testament text on the second coming of Christ. If the rapture happens in conjunction with the second coming, as posttribulationism teaches, one would expect the main biblical passage on the second coming to reference the rapture. Yet there is no mention of a rapture of saints being caught up to heaven anywhere in Revelation 19. Although this is an argument from silence, it's compelling. If the rapture is posttribulational, why is this key feature totally missing from Revelation 19? As John Walvoord notes,

> If details like the casting of the beast and the false prophet into the lake of fire are mentioned and the specific

resurrection of the tribulation saints is described, how much more the Rapture and translation of the church as a whole should have been included if, as a matter of fact, it is part of this great event. Revelation 19–20 constitutes the major problem of posttribulationists. They have no scriptural proof for a posttribulational Rapture in the very passages that ought to include it.[20]

Partial Rapture

The partial-rapture position holds that not all Christians will be raptured at the same time. This view was first articulated in the mid-1800s, and its chief proponents are Robert Govett, G.H. Lang, and D.M. Panton. According to this view, faithful, devoted believers who are watching and waiting for Christ's coming will be raptured to heaven before the tribulation begins. The rapture is viewed as a reward for faithfulness to Christ.

Support for the partial rapture view is drawn from New Testament passages that stress obedient watching and waiting for Christ such as Matthew 24:40-51; 25:1-13; Luke 20:34-36; 1 Thessalonians 5:6-10; Hebrews 9:28; Titus 2:13; 1 John 2:28; and Revelation 3:3-10. It is said that those believers who miss the first stage of the rapture will enter the tribulation and be caught up during subsequent raptures throughout the tribulation, or possibly even miss the rapture entirely. One writer described the partial rapture view like this: "All believers will go home on the same train, but not all on the first section."[21]

This view is not widely held. It's the least popular of the main rapture positions. There are several reasons we reject this view. First, the Bible consistently uses comprehensive, inclusive words like *we* and *all* when discussing the rapture. For example, 1 Corinthians 15:51 says, "*We* will not all sleep, but *we* will *all* be changed" (emphasis added). At the time that the rapture occurs, all believers will be changed, not just some. The rapture is for all true believers who are "in Christ"—no other condition is required (1 Thessalonians 4:16).

Richard Mayhue summarizes other weaknesses of this view:

> Second, a partial rapture would logically demand a parallel partial resurrection, which is nowhere taught in Scripture. Third, a partial rapture would minimize and possibly eliminate the need for the judgment seat of Christ because the group of true believers taken at the rapture receives greater reward than the group of true (but needing further spiritual refining) believers left on earth. Fourth, it creates a purgatory of sorts on earth for those believers left behind. Fifth, a partial rapture is nowhere clearly and explicitly taught in Scripture. Therefore, we conclude that the rapture will be full and complete, not just partial.[22]

Prewrath Rapture

This is the most recent of the main views. It was pioneered by Marvin Rosenthal, who wrote *The Pre-Wrath Rapture of the Church* (1990), and Robert Van Kampen, author of *The Sign* (1992). Marvin Rosenthal titled this view "prewrath rapturism."[23]

The prewrath view has four main tenets:

> The Rapture of the church will occur immediately prior to the beginning of the Day of the Lord.

> The Day of the Lord commences sometime within the second half of the seventieth week.

> The cosmic disturbances associated with the sixth seal will signal the approach of the Day of the Lord.

> The Day of the Lord will begin with the opening of the seventh seal (Rev. 8:1).[24]

This view makes a distinction between the Great Tribulation and the Day of the Lord. Rosenthal offers this summary:

The Great Tribulation will be followed by cosmic dis-
turbances, which will indicate that the Day of the Lord
is about to commence. At that time God's glory will
be manifested. Speaking broadly, "that day" will have
two objectives. First, the Rapture of the church will
occur; that will then be followed by the Lord's judgment of the wicked as He begins His physical return
to the earth.[25]

In short, prewrath rapturism contends that the rapture will transpire about three-fourths of the way through the tribulation (about
five-and-a-half years into the tribulation). The turmoil in the first
three-fourths of the tribulation is viewed as the wrath of man and
Satan, *not* the wrath of God. According to this view, the outpouring of divine wrath (the Day of the Lord) is not inaugurated until
the seventh seal judgment in Revelation 8:1. Proponents say that
believers will be raptured to heaven between the sixth and seventh
seal judgments.

While much more could be said about this view, the primary
issue is this: When does the outpouring of God's wrath begin? Pre-
wrath rapturists limit the outpouring of God's wrath and the Day
of the Lord to the final quarter of the seven-year tribulation. We
agree that the frequency and intensity of God's wrath escalates like
labor pains as the tribulation unfolds, but we believe the expression
of God's wrath begins with the first seal judgment in Revelation 6:1,
not after the sixth seal.

The judgments in Revelation 6 find parallels in Jesus's description in Matthew 24, and Jesus said all the judgments are birth pains,
which ties them all together. To say some of them are divine judgments while others are not conflicts with the words of Jesus.

Notice as well that the seal judgments in Revelation 6 are initi-
ated by the Lamb (Jesus Christ) at the very beginning of the tribulation. He's in control. They are all the outpouring of His wrath.

The seven seals, seven trumpets, and seven bowls are all divine judgments. What's more, the trumpet judgments come out of the seventh seal (Revelation 8:1). As Paul Feinberg notes, "The entire tribulation period is a time of God's wrath, from the first seal to the last bowl."[26] Paul Benware observes: "It is the Lord Jesus who breaks the seals and releases judgments on the earth. All the judgments (seals, trumpets, and bowls) come from the scroll and the One who breaks all the seals. All are demonstrations of divine wrath."[27] Scripture does not support restricting God's wrath to the trumpet and bowl judgments, as the prewrath view proposes.

Keeping Our Focus on Christ

We've covered a great deal of ground in this chapter. With that in mind, here's a simple chart that presents the big picture of all the views in one graphic:

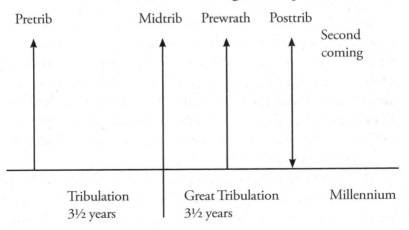

Various Views of the Timing of the Rapture

When it comes to discussing the timing of the rapture, the charitable words of Charles Ryrie serve as a great reminder for all of us. "If His coming should be pretribulational, then we will praise Him because we missed that terrible time. If it is posttribulational, then we will gladly suffer for His sake. Either way, we still have the blessed hope of His coming."[28]

May Christ always be our focus.

CHAPTER 5

History of the Rapture Doctrine

*The pretrib view...did not appear on the scene
of church history until J.N. Darby in the 1830s.*[1]

MICHAEL BIRD

The argument that the pretribulational rapture must be rejected on historical grounds must itself now be rejected. The opinion that, among earlier Christian writers, "there is no evidence of a belief that the rapture of the church would be before the tribulation" can no longer be supported by careful historians in light of overwhelming research to the contrary.[2] Historian William Watson writes, "In spite of the claims that Christian Zionism and premillennial Dispensationalism are of recent origin, very little of what John Nelson Darby wrote in the mid-nineteenth century was new."[3]

In response to the historical objections that are often raised, we will present a survey of various writers throughout history who have referred to the ideas that are germane to the pretribulation rapture. Thomas Ice emphasizes, "We need to deal with the history of the rapture not because it is a basis for determining truth, which can be found in Scripture alone, but because these issues are often at the heart of the criticisms brought against the pretribulation view."[4] We acknowledge that this view was not the dominant view of eschatology throughout most of church history, but it definitely existed long before Darby. Norman Geisler notes, "The primary question is not whether the doctrine was taught by the early church, but when it was taught by the *earliest* church—the church of the apostles."[5] Thus, within this book are some chapters that provide biblical expositions of the major rapture passages to substantiate the apostolic authors' original intent. And, we examine the rapture doctrine in light of its broader theological setting.

In this chapter, we will survey various historical references to the rapture, thus establishing these significant facts: (1) Christians have long believed in the fact that there will be a rapture; (2) the earliest Christian writers believed in the imminent return of Christ; (3) most of them were premillennial; and (4) there are multiple examples of belief in a pretribulational rapture prior to 1830, or prior to Darby.

Early Belief in the Rapture

The concept of the rapture is clearly indicated in 1 Thessalonians 4:13-18. If the Bible is accurate, there must be a time when the "dead in Christ" will be raised and living believers will be "caught up." The eschatological debate is not about whether there will *be* a rapture, but *when* it will occur. The apostle Paul described it as being "caught up" (Greek, *harpazō*) and "gathered together" (Greek, *episunagogue*). Early Christian writers spoke of the imminent coming of Christ to help them escape from great tribulation (*Shepherd of Hermas*, 1.4.2). "Watch for your life's sake...Be ready, for ye know not the hour in which our Lord cometh" (*The Didache*, 16.1, circa AD 120–150). Irenaeus spoke of the church being "suddenly caught up."[6] While their comments were not fully developed, it has often been observed that they were "seeds from which the doctrine of the Pretribulational rapture could be developed."[7] Even posttribulationalist J. Barton Payne admits that the early fathers believed in the imminent coming of Christ. He writes, "Belief in the imminence of the return of Jesus was the uniform hope of the early church."[8]

Various comments by early church fathers indicate a sense of imminence about the Savior's coming. Clement of Rome (c. AD 35–101) said, "Speedily will He come, and not tarry." Ignatius of Antioch (d. AD 110) said of Christ's coming, "Be watchful, possessing a sleepless spirit." In the *Epistle of Pseudo-Barnabas* (circa AD 70–130) we read, "The Day of the Lord is at hand…the Lord is near." In the *The Didache* we read, "Let grave come, and let this world pass away…Maranatha. Amen." Justin Martyr (AD 100–165) said, "There will be a resurrection of the dead, and a thousand years in Jerusalem."[9]

The Apocalypse of Elijah is a third-century treatise about the end times that has been reconstructed from various Greek and Coptic fragments. Francis Gumerlock, a professor of historical theology at Providence Theological Seminary in Denver, Colorado, points to it as an early example of the rapture before judgment. He notes, "As new [literary] finds are discovered, evangelicals are gradually becoming aware that pretribulationalism has a much broader history than its articulations over the last two hundred years."[10] The text was produced by a chiliast (millenarian) Christian community living in Egypt. In 5:2-6 the text describes living believers being "removed from the wrath" and taken to heaven where the "lawless one" will "have no power over them."[11] Gumerlock observes the purpose of this rapture is "specifically removal from the wrath of the Antichrist and escape from the tribulation sent on the world by God in the last days."[12]

Gumerlock also points to several early medieval writers who believed that true Christians would be raptured to heaven before the great fiery conflagration prior to the millennium.[13] He specifically mentions the anonymous *Second Apocalypse of John* (sixth to eighth century), Hilary of Poitiers (c. 315–367/368), the Venerable Bede (673–735), pseudo Alcuin (eighth or ninth century), and the Lismore version of the *Life of St. Brendan* (tenth or eleventh century).

Pseudo-Ephraem, a Syrian church father (fourth to seventh

century), provided a clear explanation of a rapture before the return, an interval between these events (in this case, three-and-a-half years), and a promise to remove believers before the tribulation ("time of confusion").[14] The sermon says:

> We ought to understand thoroughly therefore, my brothers, what is imminent...and prepare ourselves for the meeting of the Lord Jesus Christ...For all the saints and elect of God are gathered together before the tribulation, which is to come, and are taken to the Lord.[15]

While this was not the dominant medieval Catholic view, Pseudo-Ephraem's comments certainly indicate that these ideas clearly existed long before Darby—in this case, more than 1,000 years earlier. During those centuries, the Bible was not readily available to the average person, but for those who did have access to it, there was a constant stream of eschatological interpretation.

In the fourteenth century, a group known as the Apostolic Brethren flourished in northern Italy even under severe persecution. They were led by Gerard Sagarello (d. 1300), and later by Brother Dolcino (d. 1307). An anonymous treatise called *The History of Brother Dolcino*, written in Latin in 1316, explains that he believed he and his followers would be transferred into paradise and preserved unharmed from the antichrist and later descend back to the earth. He spoke of this using the Latin word *transferrentur*, which is the same word that was used by medieval Christians to describe the rapture of Enoch to heaven.[16]

Rise of Millennial Expectation

At the initial phase of the Reformation, the major reformers—like John Calvin and Martin Luther—were basically amillennial in eschatology. Nevertheless, Calvin understood Paul to teach the imminent coming of Christ. In his commentary on 1 Thessalonians,

Calvin said, "Paul...put himself, as it were, among those who will be alive at the last day. He did this to arouse the Thessalonians to wait for this last day. In addition, Paul taught this doctrine so they would be *prepared* for Christ's *return* at any moment."[17]

John Bale (1495–1563)

As persecution arose against the Reformers, many, like John Bale, fled to the European continent. A Carmelite historian turned evangelical playwright and polemicist, Bale wrote the first English-language commentary on the book of Revelation, entitled *The Image of Both Churches*. Though essentially a dramatist, historian, and martyrologist, Bale viewed the world around him through the eyes of his understanding of Revelation.[18] Like so many Reformers, he viewed papal Rome as Babylon and the woman in Revelation 12 as the true church. His awareness of the structure of Revelation led him to suggest a sevenfold pattern of history from Adam to Christ to the sixteenth century.[19]

Bale divided the seven eras based upon the seven heads of the dragon in Revelation 12: (1) serpent (Eden-Flood); (2) calf (OT idolatry); (3) lion (Assyrians and Chaldeans); (4) bear (Medes and Persians); (5) leopard (Greeks); (6) beast (Romans); and (7) man (papacy). While these certainly do not line up with later dispensational thought, they provide evidence of an early attempt to distinguish eras of time during which God dealt with humankind in different ways.

For the most part, Bale was a historian. His true interest lay in the past. However, he clearly saw the future as a projection of a sequence of past events that he believed were coming to a climax in his lifetime.

Throughout the sixteenth century, both scholarly and popular speculation continued with regard to the end of the world. In 1548, George Joye, a colleague of William Tyndale, published his translation of Andreas Osiander's *Conjectures of the Ende of the Worlde*.[20]

In it, Osiander suggested that 6,000 years of human history would be followed by a millennium of the golden age, which he identified with the church.[21] In the meantime, the immense popularity of the Geneva Bible (1560) and John Foxe's *Actes and Monuments* (1563), popularly known as *Foxe's Book of Martyrs*, brought Bale's chronological framework to life for the common English people. Events contemporary to that time, such as the excommunication of Elizabeth I and the attempted invasion by the Spanish Armada, only further heightened the general apocalyptic expectation.[22] The defeat of the Armada, which had been dispatched with the pope's blessing to bring England back into the Roman fold, left an indelible impression on the mind of Elizabethan England. It was the single most important event that persuaded the Protestant Reformers of the potential immediate fulfillment of end-times Bible prophecies.

John Napier (1550–1617)

Before the full expression of millennialism developed in Britain, many writers began to suggest a future golden age that would include the defeat of the false church and the conversion of the Jewish people to Christianity. In 1593, John Napier, a Scottish mathematical genius who invented logarithms, published *A Plaine Discovery of the Whole Revelation of Saint John*, which was replete with chronological tables. Having been influenced by the annotations in the Geneva Bible and by John Knox's colleague Christopher Goodman at St. Andrews, Napier brought academic credibility to eschatological speculation.[23]

Robert Pont (1524–1606)

Following Napier's lead, Robert Pont, John Knox's son-in-law, published *A Newe Treatise of the Right Reckoning of the Yeares and Ages of the World* in 1599. He suggested that world history could be divided into six ages, followed by the millennium, or the kingdom age.[24] His unique contribution was the idea that a seventh millennium of peace on earth would follow six millennia of human conflict:

1. Creation to Noah

2. Noah to Abraham

3. Abraham to Solomon

4. Solomon to Christ

5. Christ to 1056

6. 1056 to the end

7. Kingdom age

Hugh Broughton (1549–1612)

Considered the greatest of the Puritan Hebraists, Broughton sought to reconcile rabbinic writings with Christian revelation. In 1588 he predicted the defeat of the Spanish Armada and published *A Concent of Scripture*, in which he viewed Daniel as prophesying about world monarchies that held power over the Jewish people, and John as predicting the rise of the antichrist against the church. He later published commentaries on Daniel (1596) and Revelation (1610), in which he expressed great concern for the conversion of the Jews. However, his calculation that Christ would return in 2072 was not well received.[25]

Thomas Brightman (1557–1607)

Building on the ideas of Bale, Foxe, and Broughton, Brightman wrote his *Apocalypsis Apocalypseous* (*A Revelation of the Revelation*) in isolation in his country parish in Bedfordshire.[26] It was published in 1609, two years after his death. Intrigued by the "sevens" of the apocalypse, he suggested the seven churches of Revelation "prophesied" the seven ages of church history as follows:

Church	Period
Ephesus	Apostolic to Constantine
Smyrna	Constantine to Gratian
Pergamum	382–1300
Thyatira	1300–1520
Sardis	German Reformation
Philadelphia	Genevan Reformation
Laodicea	Church of England

Brightman's writings gave the millenarian Puritans a classic systematic exposition that would lay a foundation for many of the concepts that later influenced classic dispensationalism. Beyond that, Brightman was guilty of excessive speculations, believing the Battle of Armageddon would take place in Geneva and that Queen Elizabeth was the "first blast of the seventh trumpet."[27] He did; however, clearly indicate his belief that converted Jews would have a literal kingdom on earth involving the "full restoration of the Jewish nation."[28] Unlike earlier reformers, Brightman maintained a positive perspective toward the Jews, whom he called "our brethren."

John Henry Alsted (1588–1638)

Known in his native Germany as Johann Heinrich, John attended the Synod of Dort in 1618–1619 and was a professor of philosophy and theology at Herborn. His written works included two encyclopedias and his famous thrice-titled treatise on the millennium, first published in Germany in 1618 and posthumously translated into English in 1643 as *The Beloved City: or, the Saints Reign on Earth a Thousand Yeares.*[29] The popular influence of his work in England increased the expectation of a literal millennial reign of Christ on the earth in the future. Thus, Alsted placed several events into the future which had previously been viewed as being in the past, especially the binding of Satan and the saints' millennial reign.

Joseph Mede (1586–1638)

The leading premillennialist of the seventeenth century, Joseph Mede, was a professor of Greek at Cambridge. His views were expounded in his *Calvis Apocalypticae* (*The Key to the Revelation*), which first appeared in Latin in 1627 and was reprinted in 1632 and 1642 and translated into English in 1643. The Latin editions were intended for a small circle of intellectuals. However, the English edition took the general public by storm and instantly became the most influential premillennial book in England during that time. Mede's premillennial ideas were adopted by several members of the Westminster Assembly of Divines, including Stephen Marshall, Thomas Goodwin, Jeremiah Burroughs, and William Bridge.[30] Around the same time, Alsted's *Beloved City* (1643) appeared in English, as did John Archer's *The Personall Reign of Christ upon Earth* (1642).

In many ways, Mede was a forerunner of later dispensational eschatology. He believed in the bodily resurrection of the saints, the conversion of the Jewish people, the literal return of Christ, His 1,000-year reign upon the earth, two judgments separated by 1,000 years, and the reign of the bride of Christ (the church) during the millennium. Mede's influence was extensive. He taught John Milton, Isaac Newton, and Nathaniel Holmes and carried on extensive correspondence with Bishop James Ussher, on whom he had a great influence.[31]

Thomas Goodwin (1600–1680)

During the persecution of the Puritans by the English archbishop Charles Land, Goodwin fled to Arnhem in the Netherlands, where he helped John Archer pastor an English church. He later returned to England as one of the dissenting brethren at the Westminster Assembly. Later he became president of Magdalene College, Oxford, from 1650–1660. In 1639 he preached a series of sermons on the apocalypse, later published as *An Exposition of the Revelation*. In 1640 he preached a series on Ephesians, in which he outlined his belief that

Christ must rule on earth in a future millennium to fulfill his glory in a kingdom that combines all the people of God of all time.[32]

On a fast-day in Holland in 1641, Goodwin preached his now-famous sermon *A Glimpse of Syons Glory*.[33] Expanding his belief that Christ must reign on earth in a full manifestation of His glory, Goodwin developed a doctrine of a literal future millennium based upon a literal interpretation of passages such as Zechariah 12:10, Matthew 26:29, and Revelation 20. Thus, the stage was set for the spread of the belief in a literal return of Christ to rule in a literal millennial kingdom on earth.

Historian William Watson observes, "What occurred in the early seventeenth century was a move from medieval Roman Catholic millennialism to premillennialism."[34] Instead of viewing the millennium as the golden age of the church, the Protestant Reformers began to view the millennium as the future reign of Christ on earth. The combination of the Huguenot wars in France (1562–1598), the Spanish Armada's attempt to invade England in 1588, the Gunpowder Plot in England in 1605, and the Thirty Years' War in Europe (1618–1648) fueled a surge of apocalyptic speculation that drove the English Reformers to search the Scriptures in an attempt to understand biblical prophecies regarding the last days.

Incipient Dispensationalism

The idea of a pretribulational rapture has often been connected to the concept of dispensationalism. The concept of dispensations (Greek, *oikonomia* = "economy" or "stewardship") to divide periods of God's dealings with the human race also began to be developed in the seventeenth century. In 1647, Thomas Manton, rector of Covent Garden, preached before the House of Commons and suggested four "dispensations": (1) Law Natural, (2) Laws of Tables, (3) Gospel, (4) Latter Days.[35]

William Sherwin (1607–1687) elaborated the concept of dispensations in *The Saints Rising*, which he called "God's economy, or ordering in his household…in regard of his mercies."[36] He believed the true church would be rescued out of the world from the future "destruction," as were Noah and Lot in earlier times. In 1675, William Cave suggested three dispensations in *Antiquitates Apostolicae*: Patriarchal, Mosaical, and Evangelical in *Antiquitates Apostolicae*. Dutch theologians Hugo Grotius and Johannes Cocceius called them Promise, Law, and Gospel.[37]

Exiled French Huguenot pastor Peter Jurieu, who resided in Rotterdam, also divided history into seven periods or dispensations. Assuming six periods were ultimately given over to Satan and ended in destruction, he suggested "how much more reasonable it is to conceive, that God, after having abandoned six periods to the World and the Dragon, have at least reserved one seventh to himself."[38] French mystic Pierre Poiret published *The Divine Œconomy* in French in 1687. It was translated into English in 1713. He divided human history into seven dispensations of God's "diverse external Laws and ordinances at various times":[39]

1. Creation to the Deluge

2. Deluge to Moses

3. Moses to the Prophets

4. Prophets to Christ

5. Church Age

6. Universal Providence

7. The Millennium

The Quaker William Penn (1644–1687) wrote a work that was published posthumously in 1694, entitled, *Divers Dispensations of God to Men from the Beginning of the World to that of Our Present Age*. In it he sought to suggest that history be divided into various "dispensations of God"—from the creation in "Innocency" to the "dispensation of the Son of God" and that of the Spirit.[40] In 1699, John Edwards (1637–1716), a leading English Calvinist, wrote *A Complete History or Survey of All the Dispensations and Methods of Religion*, in which he used the term *dispensations* to mean epochs of sacred history, which he divided as follows:[41]

1. Innocence

2. Fall

3. Sacrifices

4. Noachial

5. Abrahamic

6. Mosaic

7. Christian

William Watson, when he summarized his extensive survey of the use of the term *dispensation* in the 200 years before Darby, he wrote,

> The use of the word "dispensation" was not unknown to theological authors of the seventeenth century. That it would be used by Darby and his followers is not a discontinuity of eschatological thought as so often portrayed. To the contrary, it is a continuity. The term was used in more than one way, but it cannot be said or implied that Dispensationalism arose in a vacuum or as a theological anomaly.[42]

The Rapture Before Darby

Upon reading most critics of the pretribulation rapture view, a person would get the impression that no one ever mentioned the rapture prior to 1830. But this is simply not the case. As the

Protestant Reformation spread, believers began to read and study the Bible for themselves. As they wrestled with biblical texts about the return of Christ, they began to note references to the rapture of the saints. Historian William Watson spent hundreds of hours reading obscure Puritan authors of the sixteenth, seventeenth, and eighteenth centuries and discovered numerous references to the rapture. He provides the following chart:[43]

USES OF ENGLISH WORDS/CONCEPT OF RAPTURE		
"Rapt"	"Rapture"	"Left Behind"
Vernon Manuscript 1320s?	Joseph Mede 1627	Robert Maton 1624
John Lydgate 1420	Nathaniel Homes 1653	Thomas Vincent 1667
William Bond 1531	Capt. John Browne 1654	Author of Theopolis 1672
Thomas Draxe 1613	William Sherwin 1665–1700	Oliver Heywood 1700
Barton Holyday 1626	Increase Mather 1700	Thomas Pyle 1715
George Walker 1638	Cotton Mather 1726	Grantham Killingworth 1761
William Sherwin 1665	John Norris 1738	
Joseph Hall 1708	Philip Doddridge 1739	
	John Gill 1748	
	Thomas Broughton 1768	

Watson states that "the word 'rapture' appears after the early seventeenth century, not only to refer to personal mystical experiences, but also to refer to the act of being swept bodily into heaven."[44] As early as 1626, more than two hundred years before Darby, Barton Holyday, a royal chaplain to Charles I, referred to Elijah and the "rapture of his bodie."[45] As early as 1608, Thomas Draxe (d. 1618) referred to God saving Noah and his family from the deluge and Lot from Sodom and quoting Luke 21:36, exhorting his readers to "watch and pray that we may be accounted worthy to *escape* all those things that shall come."[46] In 1627, Joseph Mede also referred to Noah as an illustration of the "rapture" and used the term six times in a single letter referring to the saints meeting the Lord in the air.[47]

In 1642, Robert Maton published both *Israel's Redemption... Our Saviour's Kingdom on Earth* and *Gog and Magog, or the Battle of the Great Day of God Almightie.* In these works, he emphasized his belief that the rapture of the living and the resurrection of the dead, with the ungodly "left behind" to experience the wrath of God, would take place before Christ's coming with His saints to rule on earth. He referred to the rapture as the time when the "elect meete the Lord in the aire."[48] He pictured Christ's coming for His saints in a time of "general security" (eating, drinking, marrying, and giving in marriage). He also predicted the Jewish people would return to their own land and that the Battle of Armageddon would take place in Judea sometime later in a time of great distress. Also in 1642 John Archer (1598–1682) published *The Personall Reign of Christ on Earth.* He too believed Christ would raise up the saints first, take them to heaven, and then return with them after a "middle state betwixt glory and mortality."[49]

Watson also points to Ephraim Huit, founder of the first church in Connecticut in 1639, who believed the "coming of the Son of Man in thee Cloudes" would save the elect from "trials." Huit explains the rapture as "the summoning of the Elect by the sound of a trumpet...heard only by the Elect."[50] Watson further notes the expectation that the saints would be taken out of the tribulation and protected from the wrath of the antichrist was common in the seventeenth century.[51] He refers to Elizabeth Avery, who wrote in 1647,

"The day shall come as a thief in the night...those that are risen at the coming of Christ, with those who are risen from the dead, shall be caught up in the clouds, to meet the Lord in the air."[52] Nathaniel Holmes (1599–1692) said, "The resurrection of those which slept in Christ, and the rapture of those which shall be left alive, together with them in the aire, should be at one and the same time."[53]

In 1654, Captain John Browne (1627–1677?), a member of the Baptist congregation in Orpington, Kent, published a detailed order of events for the "last Days." He advocated what would now be considered a midtribulation/premillennial rapture. Watson surveys Browne's eschatological chronology as follows:[54]

1. Falling away of the churches

2. Rise of the mystical Babylon

3. Division of the old Roman Empire

4. Preaching of the gospel of the kingdom

5. Calling of Judah and Benjamin

6. Rebuilding the Jewish temple

7. Revealing the Man of Sin

8. Breaking the covenant with Israel

9. Flight of the Jews into the wilderness

10. Rapture of the saints

11. Return of the ten tribes

12. 144,000 on earth

13. Great Tribulation

In 1665, William Sherwin (1607–c. 1687), wrote, "The saints... at the sounding of the last trumpet shall...be rapt up to meet Christ in the air."[55] Like many of his time, Sherwin attempted to sort out the order of the events that will take place during the last days. In

1671 he published *The Coming of Christ's Glorious Kingdom*, in which he indicated "we may expect Christ's coming very shortly."[56] A contemporary of Sherwin, Thomas Vincent (1634–1678), also expected the coming of Christ at any time, citing, as Watson notes, the very same passages about the rapture as modern dispensationalists (Matthew 24:31; John 5:28; 1 Thessalonians 4:16; Revelation 20:13).[57] Vincent wrote of the dead and living saints being "suddenly caught up together in the clouds to meet the Lord in the air" and then commented on unbelievers who will be fearful and amazed "when they perceive themselves to be left behind."[58] In the American colonies, Samuel Hutchinson (1590–1667) commented on the "time of trouble," noting, "When we see the people of God in such distress as ever was known in the world, then we may look for Christ's appearance for the delivering of them." In so doing, he clearly differentiated between Christ's glorious spiritual appearance at the rapture and His personal visible appearance at Armageddon.[59]

By 1676, Joshua Sprigg, a London rector and steward of New College Oxford, clearly expected two phases (or comings) of Christ. He said, "One of them holds forth a gradual coming…(it) is Christ's spiritual and powerful coming and appearance to the saints that is the great object of our expectation."[60] Commenting on Revelation 3:10, Sprigg believed the raptured saints would have "the first mercy, as they shall have the first fruits of his creatures, so they shall have the first fruits of redemption."[61] Watson writes, "What would follow, according to Sprigg, was non-believing Jews returning to their own land, Gog and Magog invading, the battle of Armageddon, and seven years of cleaning up the corpses and weapons before New Jerusalem descends to earth and the Millennium begins."[62]

Samuel Petto (1624–1711), an English Congregationalist pastor, published *The Revelation Unveiled* in 1693, in which he clearly distinguished the timing difference between the rapture at the beginning of the tribulation from Christ's second coming to earth to begin the millennium. According to Watson, "Petto connected the rapture to heaven with the preparation of the Bride and conversion of the Jews who will see Christ in the air."[63]

In 1690, William Lloyd published a dissertation on Daniel's 70 weeks, suggesting the "septenaries of years" (70 x 7 = 490) began with the command of Artaxerxes to rebuild Jerusalem and ended with the Messiah being "cut off," leaving one "week" of seven years yet to be fulfilled.[64] Watson notes that prior to this time, no one appears to have previously identified the tribulation period with the seventieth "week" of Daniel 9.[65] The concept of the seven years of tribulation is generally held by most pre, mid, and posttribulationalists based on a similar computation.

In America, pretribulationalism began to find expression in several prominent churchmen. Increase Mather (1639–1723), one of the most prominent Puritan pastors in colonial New England, published *The Blessed Hope, and the Glorious Appearing of the Great God Our Saviour, Jesus Christ* in 1701. He emphasized Christ's coming first to take believers to heaven to sit with Him in heavenly places before returning to earth with Him at His glorious appearing. He wrote that "when Christ comes, believers shall see the King…in all his glory and go with him to…Heaven…Christ assured believers it shall be thus, John 14:2…they will sit together with him in heavenly places…[later] they shall come down from Heaven…They shall be with him when he comes to Judge the World."[66]

Perhaps the clearest pretribulational statement prior to Darby comes from Morgan Edwards (1722–1795), who later helped found Rhode Island College, which eventually became Brown University. While a student at Bristol Baptist Seminary in the 1740s, he wrote an academic paper proposing a pretrib rapture prior to a three-and-a-half-year tribulation. Edwards wrote,

> [T]he dead saints will be raised, and the living changed at Christ's appearing in the air (I Thes iv, 17); and this will be about three years and a half before the millennium,

as we shall see hereafter; but will he and they abide in the air or one of those many "mansions in the Father's house" (John xiv.2), and so disappearing during the fore-said period of time. The design of this retreat and disappearing will be to judge the risen and changed saints; for "now the time is come that judgement must begin at the house of God" (I Pet. Iv.17).[67]

Even Jonathan Edwards (1703–1758), a postmillennialist, believed in the rapture before the final conflagration. Reading his description of the rapture reveals the sincerity and seriousness with which he viewed it:

> Upon this, Christ and all his saints, and all the holy angels ministering to them, shall leave this lower world, and ascend toward the highest heavens…he shall ascend with his elect church with him, glorified in body and soul…The redeemed church shall ascend with him in a most joyful and triumphant manner, and all their enemies and persecutors shall be left behind to be consumed.[68]

One will find an attitude of respect, devotion, and appreciation for the concept of the rapture among Protestant Reformers and Puritans even when they disagreed on the timing of the event. We refer to Watson's extensive study in his *Dispensationalism Before Darby* for numerous details and examples. He concludes this section of his study stating, "In the late eighteenth century, more than a generation before Darby, belief in a rapture of the church before a great tribulation was commonplace in Britain."[69] While the pretribulational view was not the dominant view throughout church history, it certainly existed before its codification by Darby in the 1830s.

Pretribulationism's Long History

What becomes evident from a detailed study of prophetic, apocalyptic, and eschatological writings over the centuries since the Reformation is the sincere attempt of Christians to interpret the details of biblical prophecies and formulate them into a coherent system. In fact, this was true of a wide range of biblical doctrines, including such matters as justification by faith and the nature and extent of the atonement.

With Johannes Gutenberg's innovative idea of using moveable type on a printing press, the mass-production of books became possible, and the Bible became available to a much wider audience than ever before. As a result of the Protestant Reformation, long-neglected Scriptures were read and studied by ministers and laymen alike who rediscovered apostolic teachings that had been lost to the church for centuries since the time of the apostles.

The basic doctrines of the Reformation were formulated from the Reformers' intense desire to study, interpret, and apply the truths of Scripture. As a result, those doctrines became the fuel for the fires of revival that swept Europe and America in the centuries that followed. In time, the Reformers and their theological descendants began to formulate a more biblical understanding of the Christian gospel and its implications for both the present and the future.

Today, long-forgotten works are being rediscovered that clearly indicate that the basic concepts of pretribulationism existed throughout church history long before 1830. The very issues that Darby and the earlier dispensationalists wrestled with had been swirling around in England since the sixteenth century, and previously for several centuries on the European continent. In light of this evidence, it can no longer be said that the basic concept of a pretribulational rapture was unknown before J.N. Darby. In fact, it had already been around for centuries—actually, since the time of Christ and the apostles.

CHAPTER 6

The Rapture and the Return

In short, the rapture is the first stage or phase of the second coming. The rapture and second coming are not two separate events. They are two stages of one event.[1]

GLENN KREIDER

One of the major critiques of the pretribulation rapture is that it teaches two second comings of Christ. Posttribulationists strongly object to the notion that the rapture of the church and the return of Christ to earth are two stages or phases of one event separated by at least seven years because they contend that this is teaching two future comings of Christ, while the Bible presents only one event.[2] However, the first coming of Christ included multiple events (or phases): His birth, life, ministry, death, resurrection, and ascension. In fact, His spirit left His body at His death and returned at His resurrection (Luke 23:46). This is not considered a separate coming, even though these events were separated by three days.

Of course, the same criticism can be leveled against the midtrib or prewrath views (but with these views, the time between the rapture and second coming is cut to three-and-one-half years or about a year and a half). In this chapter, we'll focus only on the pretrib response to the posttrib objection. The issue at hand is whether the coming of Jesus will occur in one event or in two stages of one event (often called the rapture and the return). Glenn Kreider clearly states the pretrib position with regard to a two-stage coming of Christ:

> The first stage of the second coming, the rapture, occurs without warning and without signs. The second stage occurs seven years later…The Day of the Lord will be bookended by the two stages of the return of Christ. In other words, the Day of the Lord begins after the rapture and concludes with the physical return of Christ to the earth to establish the eternal kingdom.[3]

So the basic question before us is this: Is it valid to view the rapture and the return as two stages of one event? Let's examine the evidence.

The Vocabulary of the Second Coming

Posttribulationists point to the terminology used in reference to the coming of Christ to bolster their view that it is one event. Because the same terms appear to be used interchangeably for Christ's coming, they reject any attempt to separate this event into two stages. Charles Ryrie states the issue concisely: "Do the words used for the second coming in the New Testament indicate that it will be a single event (posttrib view), or do they describe two events separated by seven years (pretrib view)?"[4] Referring to the posttrib argument, Ryrie continues: "To put their argument another way: since New Testament writers use several words to describe the second coming, if the rapture and return are separate events, why did they not reserve one word for the rapture and another for the return, instead of apparently using the words interchangeably?"[5]

The three main Greek words used in the New Testament in reference to Christ's coming are *parousia*, *epiphaneia*, and *apokalupsis*. *Parousia* means "coming," "arrival," or "presence." This word is found fifteen times in the New Testament, including Matthew 24:27, 1 Thessalonians 3:13, 1 Thessalonians 4:15, and 2 Thessalonians 2:8.

Epiphaneia is used in reference to the second coming five times. It means "manifestation." Among other passages, we find this word in 2 Thessalonians 2:8, 1 Timothy 6:14, 2 Timothy 4:8, and Titus 2:13.

Apokalupsis occurs five times and means "revelation" or "unveiling" (1 Corinthians 1:7; 2 Thessalonians 1:6-7; 1 Peter 1:7; 4:13; Revelation 1:1).

In support of the posttrib view, based on the vocabulary used to speak of Christ's coming, George Eldon Ladd says,

> Certainly if one can make anything of language at all, no distinction can be made between the Parousia, the apocalypse and the epiphany of our Lord. They are one and the same event...The Parousia, the apocalypse, and the epiphany appear to be a single event. And division of Christ's coming into two parts is an unproven inference...It is in other words an artificial and impossible distinction. Christ's Parousia is His return; His return is His coming; His coming is His second advent. The vocabulary used of our Lord's return lends no support for the idea of two comings of Christ or of two aspects of His coming. On the contrary, it substantiates the view that the return of Christ will be a single, indivisible glorious event.[6]

We believe this is a fair argument, but we don't believe it's a convincing one.

There is biblical precedent for one event to unfold in several stages. For example, there were three phases to the Babylonian captivity of Judah: 605, 597, and 586 BC. Each is called the captivity, but they are various stages of one event.[7] It's important to remember that there were multiple aspects or phases of Christ's first coming: His birth, His life, His death, His resurrection, and His ascension. These events were all part of the first coming and were separated by periods of time. In the same way, we believe there are two aspects of the Lord's second advent: the *rapture*, which takes place in the air, and the *return*, which begins in the air but ends with a return to earth.

Likewise, the Day of the Lord came upon Judah and various Gentile nations in the Old Testament, and the final Day of the Lord won't come until the end times.[8] Even in the end times, the Day of the Lord will be divided into a judgment phase (the Great Tribulation) and a blessing phase (the millennium). The Day of the Lord has multiple phases.

The pattern of a two-stage or two-phase coming of Christ is duplicated in the future kingdom of God, which also unfolds in two stages. Phase one is the millennial (1,000-year), messianic, earthly kingdom of Jesus as described in Revelation 20:1-6, and phase two is the eternal kingdom in the new heaven and new earth (Revelation 21:1–22:5). These are *not* two different kingdoms. They are closely connected, but they are two stages of the one glorious kingdom of God.[9] Similarly, the rapture is the initial stage of the second coming, followed by the return seven years later. They are not two different comings any more than there will be two Days of the Lord or two future kingdoms. They're two stages—one event, two stages.

Charles Ryrie provides a practical illustration concerning use of the same or similar terms in different contexts.

> ...the posttribulationists' underlying assumption in continuing to use this argument is that these words *catalog* rather than *characterize*. To be sure, vocabulary might do that; but to be equally sure, it might not.
>
> Take the word *motor*. Our washing machine has a motor. Our furnace fan has a motor. My camera has a motor that automatically advances the film. Is the term *motor* a characterizing feature of these diverse products? Or is it a means of cataloging them, which would force

us to conclude everything that has a motor is the same thing? The answer is obvious.[10]

Clearly, then, the vocabulary alone does not prove either a pre- or postrib view of the rapture. Even some postrib proponents admit this argument is not conclusive.[11] Why, then, does the vocabulary continue to be used to refute a two-stage coming? Simply because posttribulationists believe that it is a valid support that substantiates their view.

Pretribulationists believe these three words used for Christ's coming characterize different stages of one event as employed in their various contexts. If this is true, then there should be evidence in Scripture that these two phases have significant differences that cannot be reconciled. We believe there is.

The Variations Between the Rapture and the Return

While the vocabulary of the second coming doesn't move the needle in favor of any view regarding the timing of the rapture, the fact there are distinctly different descriptions about what happens during the second coming tilts the discussion in favor of the pretribulation position. The dissimilarities that exist between the accounts of Christ's coming override the similarity that's present in the vocabulary. These dissimilarities are significant enough that the only sensible explanation is that the second coming has two phases (the rapture and the return).

There are three main rapture passages in the New Testament: John 14:1-3, 1 Corinthians 15:51-55, and 1 Thessalonians 4:13-18. Among the principal second coming passages are Zechariah 14:1-21, Matthew 24:29-31, Mark 13:24-27, Luke 21:25-27, and Revelation 19:11-21. The differences between these two groups of passages are striking. They are so striking that they clearly point to two separate contexts.

Certainly, there are some similarities between the rapture and the return. Both events mention a coming, and both mention clouds, symbolizing a heavenly role in both. Yet the differences demonstrate that these are two distinct stages of the second coming. John Walvoord notes, "While it is evident that there are some similarities in the two events, these do not prove that they are the same. There are similarities also between the first and the second coming of Christ, but these have been separated by almost two thousand years."[12] Similarities exist between the rapture and the return, but the irreconcilable dissimilarities carry more weight.

Here are some of the more significant differences between the rapture and the return as they are described in Scripture.[13]

There is a difference in the signs given for each stage.

Before the rapture—There are no signs that must take place. The rapture can happen at any moment. It's a signless event. None of the rapture passages contain any mention of preceding signs. Believers are enjoined to be constantly looking for the rapture and "to wait" for it (1 Thessalonians 1:10).

Before the return—Specific signs must come to pass before Christ will return to earth (Matthew 24:4-28). The same event cannot logically be both signless and yet portended by numerous signs. That is clearly contradictory. The simplest harmonization of these two different events supports a pretribulational rapture (which is signless and could happen at any moment), while the many events taking place during the tribulation are best understood as signs leading up to the second coming.

There is a difference in the place Christ will meet believers.

At the rapture—Christians will meet the Lord in the air (1 Thessalonians 4:16-17). Jesus never sets foot on the earth in any of the rapture texts.

At the return—Christ will come to earth with His saints, descending upon the Mount of Olives in Jerusalem (Zechariah 14:2-4; Revelation 19:14).

There is a difference in who removes people from the earth.

At the rapture—Christ Himself comes and takes believers out of the world. He comes *for* His saints (John 14:1-3; 1 Thessalonians 4:16-17).

At the return—Christ sends His angels to gather His elect on earth (Matthew 24:31).

There is a difference in who gets taken from the earth and who is left.

At the rapture—Believers are taken from the earth, while unbelievers are left behind (1 Thessalonians 4:17).

At the return—Living believers on earth are left to enter the messianic kingdom while unbelievers are take away to judgment (Matthew 13:41-42, 49-50).

There is a difference of when Jesus comes in relationship to the tribulation.

At the rapture—Jesus comes to rescue Christians *before* the time of tribulation and wrath (1 Thessalonians 1:10; Revelation 3:10).

At the return—Jesus comes *after the tribulation* to conquer His enemies, punish the wicked, and rule the world (Matthew 24:29-30).

There is a difference as to when judgment takes place.

At the rapture—No mention is made of God's judgment or any distress taking place. Only promises of blessing and salvation are referenced.

At the return—Tribulation, distress, apocalypse, and judgment are everywhere (Zechariah 14:2-4; Matthew 25:31-46; Revelation 19:11-21).

There is a difference in the timing of the resurrection of the dead.

At the rapture—The resurrection of the dead occurs during Christ's descent from heaven (1 Thessalonians 4:16-17).

At the return—A resurrection of believers who died during the tribulation takes place after Christ has descended to earth. Note the order of events in Revelation 19:11–20:5: (1) the descent of Christ; (2) Christ slays His enemies; (3) the antichrist (the beast) and the false prophet are cast alive into the lake of fire; (4) Satan is bound and thrown into the pit; (5) after all these events, there is a resurrection of the saints.

There is a difference in the people involved.

At the rapture—Only believers see Christ and are involved (John 14:1-3; 1 Thessalonians 4:16-17).

At the return—All people will see Jesus coming and are involved (Revelation 1:7; 19:11-21).

There is a difference in the mention of the rapture of living believers.

Rapture passages—All focus on the snatching away of living believers on earth to meet Jesus in the air.

Return passages—No second coming passage contains a clear, indisputable reference to the rapture. In none of the second advent passages—even the most detailed ones in Matthew 24 and Revelation 19—is there a clear mention of a catching up of living believers to meet Jesus in the air. This omission is inexplicable if the rapture and return are supposed to happen simultaneously.

There is a difference in the changes on earth associated with these events.

At the rapture—All the relevant passages are silent about any topographical changes taking place on the earth.

At the return—Massive changes in and on the earth result from Christ's coming (Zechariah 14:1-11).

This helpful chart puts the differences side by side so you can see and study for yourself whether a two-stage second coming is supported by Scripture:

The Rapture	The Return
Christ comes in the air (1 Thess. 4:16-17)	Christ descends to the earth, to the Mount of Olives in Jerusalem (Zech. 14:4)
Christ comes for His saints (1 Thess. 4:16-17)	Christ comes with His saints (1 Thess. 3:13; Jude 14)
Living believers are caught up to heaven	No mention of a rapture of living saints
Believers depart the earth (1 Thess. 4:16-17)	Unbelievers are taken away (Matt. 24:37-41)
Christ claims His bride	Christ comes with His bride
Christ gathers His own (1 Thess. 4:16-17)	Angels gather the elect (Matt. 24:31)
Christ comes to reward (1 Thess. 4:17)	Christ comes to judge (Matt. 25:31-46)
Not in the Old Testament (1 Cor. 15:51)	Predicted often in the Old Testament
There are no signs; it is imminent	Portended by many signs (Matt. 24:4-29)
It is a time of blessing and comfort (1 Thess. 4:18)	It is a time of destruction and judgment (2 Thess. 2:8-12)
Involves believers only (Jn. 14:1-3; 1 Cor. 15:51-55; 1 Thess. 4:13-18)	Involves all people on earth (Matt. 24:1–25:46)
Will occur in a moment, in the time it takes to blink—only believers will see Him (1 Cor. 15:51-52)	Will be visible to the entire world (Matt. 24:27; Rev. 1:7)

While both the rapture and the return describe a coming of the Lord and the same terms are used to refer to both, the dramatic differences in the various passages we've examined indicate they are describing two unique events that occur at separate times. The dissimilarities are too substantial to merge them into a single event. [14]

The Posttribulational Response

So how do postribulationists handle the dissimilarities that are present in passages they believe describe the same event? For the most part, they don't address all the distinctions. Ladd makes passing reference to the differences and says, "There is no ground whatsoever to assume that there must be a considerable time between the Rapture and Christ's coming with His Church. They may be two aspects of single indivisible event."[15] He argues that any notion of two separate events separated by a number of years is only an interpretation or inference and is nowhere specifically stated in Scripture.[16] Douglas Moo says:

> A posttribulationist readily concedes that the Rapture and the Second Coming in *judgment* are not identical, in the sense that they have different purposes or affect different groups of people. All that the posttribulationist affirms is that these two events are part of one complex event, the Parousia, and that it will occur after the Tribulation.[17]

Moo addresses some of the specific dissimilarities between the rapture and the return, arguing that the rapture is mentioned in conjunction with the second coming in Matthew 24:31, but he agrees this "reference is not 'indisputable.'"[18] His overall contention is that New Testament passages were addressed to specific situations, which means the author only includes what is necessary to make his point and omits details that are unnecessary to meet his immediate purpose. He believes the omissions of various aspects of Christ's coming in different texts are best understood in this way and accounts for the differences in the various passages.[19] Of course we agree that not every New Testament author gives all the details on any given matter to his intended audience, but the details cannot be *contradictory* and still describe the same event.

Moo points to the apparent inconsistencies in the Gospel narratives concerning the resurrection of Christ and says that in spite of these differences, "we know that all depict the same event."[20] Moo is correct that apparent inconsistencies in accounts of the same event can often be easily reconciled. In the Gospels, each human author has a particular audience and purpose in view and thus stresses different details surrounding the resurrection. However, every Gospel writer clearly records the fact of Jesus's resurrection. To omit that fact would be a major omission. In the same way, while different authors may give different details about the Lord's coming, for an account to omit any reference to the rapture of living believers to heaven is quite an omission. The lack of any *clear, indisputable* reference to the rapture in Matthew 24 and Revelation 19:11-21—the two main second coming texts—is tantamount to one of the Gospel writers omitting mention of the resurrection of Jesus. The failure to mention the rapture leaves us with a dissimilarity that is so great that it's a clear indicator there are two different events in view.

In addition, the Gospel accounts that describe the events of the resurrection are long narrative passages that are prone to minor differences that are easily explained and reconciled. The rapture and return passages, however, are found most often in prophetic discourse or epistolary text, which are generally not given to having significant differences between related passages.

What the Evidence Says

Are there differences between various passages describing the second coming? All agree there are. The follow-up question, then, is this: Are these dissimilarities numerous enough and noteworthy enough to warrant two stages of Christ's coming? That's the question each interpreter must answer.

We leave it to you, based on the evidence we've presented from Scripture, to decide whether the many striking dissimilarities between the rapture and the return can be reasonably explained by the suggestion that authors left out supposedly unnecessary details in various contexts. We also leave it to you to discern, based on what you have read so far, whether the pretribulation view truly does have scriptural support, or it is just an inference nowhere asserted in God's Word.

We believe the conspicuous differences in various passages dealing with the Lord's return point toward a two-phase second coming. These two stages are harmonized well by the pretribulation view, while other views of the timing of the rapture are unable to accommodate the differences as smoothly. An examination of the vocabulary used in reference to the coming of Jesus as well as the variations between the passages that describe His return supports a two-stage coming of Jesus separated by at least seven years. In support of this view, John MacArthur says,

> Scripture suggests that the Second Coming occurs in two stages—first the Rapture, when He comes *for* His saints and they are caught up to meet Him in the air (1 Thess. 4:14-17), and second, His return to earth, when He comes *with* His saints (Jude 14) to execute judgment on His enemies. Daniel's seventieth week must fall *between* those two events. That is the only scenario that reconciles the imminency of Christ's coming *for* His saints with the yet unfulfilled signs that signal His final glorious return *with* the saints.[21]

Jesus is coming again. On this point, all Christians agree. The authors of this book believe He is coming *before* the tribulation, without any advance warning, to take His bride to heaven. He can come at any moment.

Live looking!

CHAPTER 7

Bringing the Future into Focus

*Eschatology means the theology of last things...
Everyone has some sort of eschatology...But there is
much divergence in this area of doctrine, and because
some things are not crystal clear, some assume that
eschatology should be given lesser importance
than other areas of biblical truth. Is there any area
of doctrine that has not been debated?...we must
not slight what the Bible says about the future.*[1]

CHARLES RYRIE

The focus of this book is on the rapture of the church to heaven. However, to fully understand the nature of the rapture and the various views of its timing, it's helpful to get a broader picture of other issues concerning the end times. The main feature of the various elements is *timing*. The *when* question is the key issue to understanding the prophetic Scriptures. For example, in the broadest terms, *when* will the prophecies of the New Testament find fulfillment—have they already been fulfilled, are they being fulfilled, or are the majority of them yet to be fulfilled? *When* will Christ reign for 1,000 years? Is He reigning now, or should we expect a future reign on the earth? And *when* will the rapture take place? These are the key issues of eschatology.

The way people answer the *when* question is affected, to a large extent, by the approach they take to Bible prophecy. In this chapter, we're going to look at some of the different ways people approach Bible prophecy and how that influences their views on the millennium, the rapture, and other events mentioned in the prophetic scriptures.

With that in mind, let's walk through three basic steps involved in developing one's perspectives on prophecy.

Step 1: Adopting an Approach

When studying Bible prophecy, especially the book of Revelation, there are four main approaches that frame the timing of prophetic events and their fulfillment.[2] Below, we briefly explain each view and provide a succinct evaluation of it.

Preterism

The word *preterism* derives from the Latin word *praeter*, which means "past." Preterists view most or all of the prophecies in Revelation (and in other New Testament passages) as having already been fulfilled, up to and including the destruction of Jerusalem by the Romans in AD 70.

There are two main branches of preterism: partial preterism and full preterism.

R.C. Sproul, a partial preterist, defines the preterist approach as "an eschatological viewpoint that places many or all eschatological events in the past, especially during the destruction of Jerusalem in A.D. 70."[3]

Preterists believe that Jesus actually came in AD 70 in a "cloud coming" to destroy Jerusalem through the Roman army and that Nero was the "beast" described in Revelation 13. Sproul represents this view when he says, "Preterists argue not only that the kingdom is a present reality, but also that in a real historical event the *parousia* [Christ's coming] has already occurred."[4] Preterist David Chilton says,

For us, the great majority of the Revelation is *history*. It has already happened. The greatest enemy of the early Church was apostate Israel, which used the power of the pagan Roman Empire to try to stamp out Christianity... St. John's message in Revelation was that this great obstacle to the Church's victory over the world would soon be judged and destroyed. His message was contemporary, not futuristic.[5]

Other noted partial preterists are Kenneth Gentry, Jr. and Gary DeMar. They believe the time of tribulation is past—it happened in AD 70. They reject any notion of a seven-year time of Great Tribulation at the end of the age. While partial preterists believe that Jesus's coming happened in AD 70, they do believe in a final return of Jesus at the end of the age.[6]

Full preterists believe that *all* biblical prophecies—including those related to the second coming and the final resurrection of believers—have already been fulfilled. According to their system of thought, history has progressed all the way to the new heavens and new earth in Revelation 21–22. Their denial of a final, literal resurrection of the dead and final judgment puts them outside the pale of orthodoxy.

One weakness of the preterist view is its inability to maintain a consistent interpretive method with regard to Bible prophecy. Preterists apply a literal method of interpretation to passages that they can fit into the historical events that occurred in AD 70. But when they come to a prophecy that doesn't fit what happened in AD 70, they resort to interpreting the passage in a spiritual or allegorical manner. This view, then, is plagued by inconsistency.

Another problem with preterism is that it often limits the global language of prophecy ("the earth" in Revelation 68, and "all the tribes of the earth" in Revelation 1:7) to the Jewish people and land of Israel.[7]

A significant glaring weakness of preterism has to do with the date that the book of Revelation was written. Because preterists believe Revelation is a prophecy of events fulfilled that were fulfilled between AD 67 and 70, they are forced to date the book's composition at AD 65. This is the Achilles' heel of preterism. Overwhelming evidence supports Revelation as having been written in AD 95.[8] This date for the book of Revelation invalidates the preterist view as a viable option.

Historicism

The genesis of the historicist view has been traced to Joachim of Fiore in the twelfth century.[9] The historicist approach maintains that the book of Revelation outlines a prophetic panorama of the major events of church history from the first century to the return of Jesus.[10] "Historicism was popular during the Protestant Reformation as the Reformers (Luther, Calvin and Zwingli) identified the Antichrist and Babylon with the pope and Roman Catholicism of their day. This 'newspaper approach' to prophecy has led historicist interpreters to identify the Antichrist with figures like Charlemagne, Napoleon, Mussolini, and Hitler, to name just a few."[11]

The *Dictionary of Biblical Prophecy and End Times* spotlights the major weakness of historicism: "Most problematic for historicism is the complete lack of agreement about the various outlines of church history. History is like a target for those who want to read Revelation in this way, and there is no consensus about what the book means, even among interpreters within the same school of interpretation. Rather, inconsistency, conjecture, and speculation abound."[12]

Historicism is not widely held today.

Idealism

Idealism is also known as the spiritual or symbolic view. Robert Thomas calls it the "timeless-symbolic" approach.[13] Idealism "interprets Revelation as a series of repeated symbolic pictures of the church's struggle from John's day until the second coming, the last judgment, and the eternal state."[14] Idealists envision Revelation as a depiction of the battle between the church and the world at all times in church history. No concrete meaning is attached to the numerous symbols in the book.

Idealism grew out of the soil of the allegorical method of interpretation that surfaced under Philo. Origen and Clement rejected a literal method of interpretation in favor of a spiritualized meaning of the symbols. This view was later espoused by Augustine and Jerome.[15] Idealism, to at least some degree, is a growing view among both evangelical and nonevangelical scholars today.

The main criticism of idealism is that symbols in Revelation have a literal referent. They refer to something that is literal. Jesus Himself adopted this method of interpreting the symbols in Revelation chapter 1 (the seven lampstands and seven stars, see Revelation 1:20). Departing from the interpretive guide that Jesus established in Revelation 1 is unwarranted and unwise.

Futurism

Futurism contends that New Testament prophecies, including those in Revelation 4–22, refer to real people and events yet to appear on the world stage. Many luminaries in the early church were futurists: Justin Martyr, Irenaeus, Hippolytus, and Victorinus.

One of the main criticisms of futurism relates to the issue of reader relevance. Opponents argue that this view "removes Revelation from its original setting so that the book has little meaning for the original audience."[16] In other words, how can prophecies regarding the distant end times have significant relevance for readers in the first century? Greg Beale, who is not a futurist, summarizes the futurist response to this objection: "The futurist may contend that the book would have been relevant since Christ's coming has always been expected imminently and that even first-century readers could therefore have thought the visions about the 'final great tribulation' were potentially quite pertinent to them."[17]

All things considered, the futurist approach is far superior to the other views. Futurism *consistently* follows the principles of interpreting Scripture literally. Futurism stays in line with the prophecies of Daniel that speak of the end of all things. Furthermore, a reader would expect the New Testament, and especially the book of Revelation, to fill in the end of the story that began in Genesis.

Again, Step 1 has to do with adopting an overarching view with regard to the timing of prophetic events. That brings us to Step 2, which is to make a decision about the millennium, which is mentioned in Revelation 20:1-6.

Step 2: Meaning of the Millennium

The world *millennium* does not appear in the Bible, but it is of Latin origin and it means "1,000 years." This number is mentioned six times in Revelation 20:1-6. There are three major views about the timing and nature of this 1,000-year reign of Christ.

Amillennialism

Amillennialists believe the reign of Christ is going on now. The time frame of the 1,000-year reign of Christ is said to be the "whole time between Christ's first and second advents."[18]

For amillennialists, the reign of Christ is spiritual in nature—Christ reigns in heaven and in the hearts of His people. The 1,000-year time marker, referenced six times in Revelation 20:1-6, is understood symbolically. This view came into existence through Tyconius and Augustine in the early fifth century AD.

Postmillennialism

Postmillennialists hold that Jesus will return *post*—or after—the millennial kingdom has been established on earth by means of the preaching of the gospel. Like amillennialists, postmillennialists view the millennium as being present today. The main distinction is postmillennialists believe the world will become *christianized* by means of mass conversions and worldwide revival.[19] In their view, the world will steadily grow better and as the gospel message spreads, eventually culminating in a golden age. When this golden age is achieved, Christ will return to earth.

Postmillennialists date the emergence of their view as early as the twelfth century, but all agree that it was popularized and systematized by Daniel Whitby in the early eighteenth century.

Premillennialism

Premillennialists maintain that the return of Christ is premillennial (that is, before the millennium). The 1,000-year reign of Christ on earth will begin after the second coming. For premillennialists the millennium is future, literal, and on earth. Premillennialism was known in the early church as *chiliasm*, which means "1,000 years." This viewpoint was the dominant view of the early church—church historian Philip Schaff notes:

> The most striking point in the eschatology of the ante-Nicene age [AD 100–325] is the prominent chiliasm, or millennarianism, that is the belief of a visible reign of Christ in glory on earth with the risen saints for a thousand years, before the general resurrection and judgment. It was indeed not the doctrine of the church embodied in any creed or form of devotion, but a widely current opinion of distinguished teachers, such as Barnabas, Papias, Justin Martyr, Irenaeus, Tertullian, Methodius, and Lactantius.[20]

Premillennialists divide into two sub-groups: dispensational premillennialists and historic premillennialists. Steve Gregg highlights the difference between these two branches of premillennialism:

> Among those who hold to this view, there are two major varieties: the dispensational and the historic

premillennialists. The principal points of departure between these two groups is the former believe in a special status of the nation Israel in the redemptive work of God in the end times…whereas, the historic premillennarians see the church, rather than ethnic Israel, as prominent in the millennial period. Dispensationalists also are distinctive in holding that the church will be raptured out of the earth seven years prior to the commencement of the Millennium, whereas other *premillennialists* see the Rapture of the church as occurring simultaneously with the descent of Christ to earth at the establishment of the millennial order.[21]

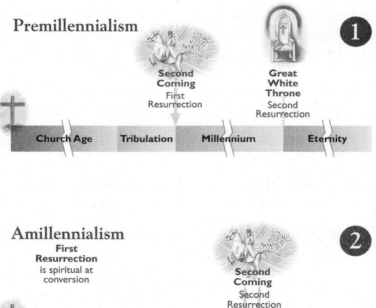

Premillennialism ❶

Second Coming
First Resurrection

Great White Throne
Second Resurrection

Church Age — Tribulation — Millennium — Eternity

Amillennialism ❷
First Resurrection
is spiritual at conversion

Second Coming
Second Resurrection
All Judgment

Church Age

Millennium

Eternity

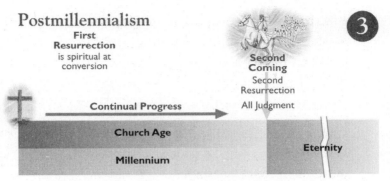

From Tim LaHaye and Thomas Ice, *Charting the End Times* (Eugene, OR: Harvest House Publishers, 2001), 129.

Step 3: Resolving the Rapture

After adopting an overall approach to the timing of prophetic fulfillment, and a view regarding the timing and nature of the millennium, the final timing decision concerns the rapture itself. There are four main views here:

- *Pretribulation*—The rapture occurs before the seven-year tribulation.

- *Midtribulation*—The rapture occurs at the midpoint of the tribulation.

- *Prewrath*—The rapture occurs three-fourths of the way through the tribulation.

- *Posttribulation*—The rapture occurs at the end of the tribulation as part of the return of Christ to earth.

These views are presented and evaluated in chapter 4.

Bringing the prophecies of the Bible into focus begins with adopting an overall approach, progresses from there to the meaning of the millennium, and culminates with determining the timing of the rapture. Now that we've walked through these steps, let's put the pieces together and see how the various views relate to one another:

- *Partial preterists* are always *amillennial* or *postmillennial* and hold to a rapture in conjunction with the return of Christ.

- *Historicists* can be *amillennial, postmillennial,* or *premillennial* and believe in a *posttribulational* rapture.

- *Idealists* are *amillennial* or *postmillennial* and hold to a *posttribulation* rapture (or at least a rapture at the same time as the second coming).

- *Futurists* are generally *premillennial* but can hold to *any of the four views* of the rapture.

We realize that the various elements of the different views may be hard to remember at first. But as you come to understand how each view approaches Bible prophecy, you'll gain a better sense for what each one says about the timing of the rapture and the millennium. And this, in turn, will help you gain a better sense for which views actually line up with Scripture as you study the many passages that have to do with Bible prophecy.

With those parameters established, let's turn our attention back to the rapture itself.

CHAPTER 8

Is the Rapture Imminent?

*As an imminent event, the rapture of the church
is the immediate expectation of those who
put their faith and trust in Jesus Christ.*[1]

MARK BAILEY

A foundational aspect of the rapture, as taught in Scripture, is that it is imminent. By *imminent* we mean it could happen at any moment, and there is no prophesied event that has to take place first before the rapture can occur. It *is* the next event on the calendar.

However, there are some who argue that the rapture or return of Christ cannot be imminent. In this chapter, we'll define *imminence*, identify the main objections to imminence, and discuss the most important Scripture passages that support the idea that the rapture could happen at any time.

Defining Imminence

In connection with the rapture, the term *imminence* is generally used to communicate an "at any moment" view of this event. Gerald Stanton notes, "As applied to the coming of the Lord, imminency consists of three things: the certainty that he may come at any moment, the uncertainty of the time of that arrival, and the fact that no prophesied event stands between the believer and that hour."[2]

New Testament scholar Robert Gundry further explains, "By

common consent imminence means that so far as we know no predicted event will *necessarily* precede the coming of Christ."[3] John Sproule adds, "Christ can return for His Church at any moment and…no predicted event will intervene before that return."[4]

Renald Showers explains, "Other events *may* happen before the imminent return, but nothing else *must* take place before it happens. If something else must take place before an event can happen, that event is not imminent."[5] Wayne Brindle adds, "Jesus can return for His church at any moment, and no predicted event must necessarily precede His return."[6]

As you can see, to suggest the rapture is imminent requires more detail than requiring the event will take place at any time. Much of the emphasis in these and other scholarly definitions of imminence have arisen from various objections to the view of an imminent rapture.

Objections to Imminence

The first common objection given against an imminent rapture is the claim that certain New Testament events had to take place before this event. If so, then the rapture could not be defined as imminent.

One example often cited is Jesus's promise to send the Holy Spirit at Pentecost: "John baptized with water, but in a few days you will be baptized with the Holy Spirit" (Acts 1:5 NIV). Opponents of an imminent rapture argue this event *had* to occur first. Therefore, the rapture could not have literally occurred at any moment. The flaw in this objection, however, is that the primary passages relating to the rapture were given *after* this Pentecost occurred. For example, 1 Thessalonians 4:13-18 was written around AD 51, approximately 20 years later.

Another New Testament event objectors cite is the prediction of Peter's death (John 21:22-23). If Jesus knew when Peter would die (approximately AD 65), then how could the rapture take place at any moment? Objectors also point to passages about the destruction of the Jewish temple (Matthew 24:2; Mark 13:2), which took place in AD 70, as well as the fact it was necessary for Paul to first preach the gospel in Rome (Acts 23:11). These and other predicted New Testament events did take place, yet do not contradict the biblical predictions of an at-any-moment rapture. A simple answer is that Jesus *could* have raptured the church at any time, yet has chosen not to do so until a yet future unknown time. This negates already-fulfilled past predictions because we are focusing on real events still to come, not hypothetical, potential contradictions from the past.

The second major objection to an imminent rapture is the view of "expectancy, not imminency." For example, Marvin J. Rosenthal writes, "There simply are no verses in the Bible which teach that Christ's return can occur at any moment, is signless, and that no prophesied events will precede it—an absolute necessity to sustain pretribulationism."[7]

Rosenthal proceeds to argue 1 Thessalonians 4:13-15 and similar passages do argue for believers to expect Christ to return in the future. However, they do not argue for an at-any-moment view. He adds, "A score of verses teach the Second Coming of Christ. All are consistent with the thesis that Christ could return in any generation."[8]

This perspective, however, simply argues the church will enter Daniel's seventieth week and endure the tribulation. It does not actually defend against the teaching that Christ could rapture believers at any moment. Rather, it combines biblical passages regarding the rapture with those referring to the second coming of Christ at the end of the tribulation. This, of course, is post-tribulationism, which expects Christ to return for His people at the *end* of the tribulation, rather than *before*. In contrast with the pretribulation view, posttribulationists say the rapture and second coming are one event. This event, even among those holding a posttribulational view, still takes place at an unknown moment in the future.

But the posttribulational idea that we can be expectant about Christ's return—without it being imminent—argues that passages related to the rapture are describing the same event as the second coming. The problem is that many distinctions exist. Thomas Ice noted the following 13 major differences in his research:

Rapture	Second Coming
1 Translation of all believers	1 No translation at all
2 Translated saints go to heaven	2 Translated saints return to earth
3 Earth not judged	3 Earth judged and righteousness established
4 Imminent, at any moment, signless	4 Follows definite predicted signs, including the tribulation
5 Not in the Old Testament	5 Predicted often in Old Testament
6 Believers only	6 Affects all men
7 Before the day of wrath	7 Concludes the day of wrath
8 No reference to Satan	8 Satan bound
9 Christ comes for His own	9 Christ comes with His own
10 He comes in the air	10 He comes to the earth
11 He claims His bride	11 He comes with His bride
12 Only His own see Him	12 Every eye shall see Him
13 Tribulation begins	13 Millennial kingdom begins[9]

Ice concludes, "The distinctions between Christ's coming in the air to rapture His church are too great to be reduced into a single coming at the end of the tribulation. These biblical distinctions provide a strong basis for the pre-trib rapture teaching."[10]

The third major objection brought up against the idea of an imminent rapture is that the rapture is said to be a modern concept that arose in the nineteenth century. Because it was not taught in the early church, objectors argue that the idea of an imminent rapture has no roots in church history and teaching. For example, Rosenthal claims, "Far from having its roots in the early church, Pretribulational Rapturism and an any-moment Rapture can trace its origin back to John Darby and the Plymouth Brethren in the year 1830."[11] Yet research shows this is far from accurate. While Darby contributed to popularizing the rapture view in recent church history, he was far from the first to develop the concept. Todd Strandberg provides four clear written examples from the church fathers—all from within the first 400 years of the church's history—that make it clear the concept of imminency has been around from early on:

- "All the saints and elect of God are gathered together before the tribulation, which is to come, and are taken to the Lord, in order that they may not see at any time the confusion which overwhelms the world because of our sins" (*Pseudo-Ephraem*, AD 374–627).

- "Of a truth, soon and suddenly shall His will be accomplished, as the Scripture also bears witness, saying, 'speedily will He come, and will not tarry.'" *The First Epistle of Clement*, 23 (written around AD 96 by Clement, a prominent leader of the church at Rome who knew some of the apostles personally and is probably the Clement referred to in Philippians 4:3).

- "Be vigilant over your life; let your lamps not be extinguished, or your loins ungirded, but be prepared, for you know not the hour in which our Lord will come" (The *Didache*, chapter 16, section 1, as early as AD 70–180).

- "But what a spectacle is that fast-approaching advent of our Lord, now owned by all, now highly exalted, now a triumphant One!" (Tertullian, AD 155–245).[12]

LaHaye quotes similar research from church history, concluding,

> There can be no doubt these fourth- (or at the latest seventh-) century Bible scholars saw the saints gathered together before the Tribulation by the coming of the Lord. His statement has all the marks of a pre-Tribulation rapture of the saints as distinct from the Glorious Appearing, which our Lord promised would occur "immediately after the distress of those days..." (Matt. 24:29).[13]

Regarding the emphasis on Darby as the originator of the imminent rapture view, LaHaye further reveals:

> Roy Huebner, a careful pre-Tribulation scholar, has proven that many saw the Rapture before John Darby first saw it in 1827. He said, "The word 'rapture' was in use, to designate the catching up of the saints, long before 1832. For example, Joseph Mede (1586–1638) wrote, 'Therefore, it is not needful that the Resurrection of those which slept in Christ, and the Rapture of those which shall be left alive together with them in the air...'"

> This clearly indicates that Mede, the great sixteenth-century literalist, understood 1 Thessalonians 4:13-18 to teach the catching up of the saints and used the term rapture to designate that catching up. His statement was made 250 years before Darby taught the Rapture! Thus, we see that the term rapture was not unique to Darby, but had been used by others before him.[14]

A fourth argument against the imminency of the rapture is that it is not explicitly taught in Scripture. "While it's true no single verse alone specifically says Jesus is coming to rapture His saints before the seven-year Tribulation, there are clear statements that He is coming to deliver His people from the coming wrath (1 Thessalonians 1:10; 5:9; Revelation 3:10). Thus, it stands to reason that God will use the Rapture to accomplish this promise."[15] This argument is insufficient, as there are other biblical doctrines, such as those concerning the Trinity and the inerrancy of Scripture, which are likewise not explicitly stated in just a single verse.

F. Kenton Beshore and R. William Keller argue that yet another reason the rapture is not imminent is because of the inconsistent writings of those who hold to a pretribulational rapture position. They said, "Joel Rosenberg, a *New York Times* best-selling author and founder of the Joshua Fund, is a strong Pre-Tribulationist who believes in *imminence*, but he thinks it is possible the Russian invasion of Israel could take place before the Rapture."[16] Based on this suggestion, they claim Rosenberg and others who hold to an imminent rapture view are inconsistent because they see certain events taking place before the rapture.

However, these authors fail to distinguish between what *could* take place and what *must* take place before the rapture. Rosenberg and others, ourselves included, realize some aspects of biblical prophecy are less certain regarding their timing and may take place either before or after the rapture. However, this doesn't mean certain events *must* occur before the rapture takes place. It only means certain events *might* take place first.

These five major areas of objection do not ultimately provide sufficient contradictory evidence to the view that the rapture is imminent. That said, let's turn to the Bible's own words regarding the evidence for imminency.

The Bible's Own Words on Imminence

The primary focus in the debate over whether the rapture is imminent should focus on which biblical passages actually address the subject. Brindle provides four important criteria that help to establish the parameters of our study:

1. The passage speaks of Christ's return as at any moment.

2. It speaks of Christ's return as near, without giving any signs preceding His coming.

3. It speaks of Christ's return as something that gives believers hope and encouragement, without indicating that these believers will suffer tribulation.

4. It speaks of Christ's return as giving hope without relating it to God's judgment of mankind.[17]

Based on these criteria, Brindle has identified seven specific Bible passages that teach, imply, or allow for an at-any-moment rapture. Here is the Bible's strongest evidence on this topic.

John 14:1-3

> Do not let your heart be troubled; believe in God, believe also in Me. In My Father's house are many dwelling places; if it were not so, I would have told you; for I go to prepare a place for you. If I go and prepare a place for you, I will come again and receive you to Myself, that where I am, there you may be also.

A quick look at these words reveals Brindle's criteria. First, Jesus Himself says He will come back at any future moment. Second, no signs are mentioned, with the exception of Jesus first leaving, a requirement necessary for Him to later return. Third, Jesus clearly indicates His return will be a time of hope rather than tribulation. Fourth, this future coming will take place without any reference to God's judgment on humanity.

Robert Dean adds another important insight regarding this rapture passage with his question, "Where do we go with the Lord when He returns?"

Thus, John 14:1-3 clearly speaks of Jesus' departure from the earthly realm to the heavenly abode of the Father. There He will prepare for the arrival of the Church and the marriage of the Bride. Following Jewish wedding customs, He will later return to the earth to take His Bride to the location He has prepared, which is not on the earth but in heaven. Once the bride is gathered, then the purification which occurs at the judgment seat of Christ follows, and then the wedding feast which occurs before the Second Coming.

This means that this future return to take believers to their heavenly abodes cannot be at the same time as the coming to the earth described in Revelation 19:7ff. In that case, Jesus would simply be catching up the bride to Himself on His way down to the earth with no time for either the Judgment Seat of Christ or the Wedding Feast. The destiny of the church then would be the earth rather than heaven. John 13:1-3 clearly tells us that our Lord will take us to heaven at His return at the Rapture.[18]

1 Thessalonians 1:9-10

They themselves report about us what kind of a reception we had with you, and how you turned to God from idols to serve a living and true God, and to wait for His Son from heaven, whom He raised from the dead, that is Jesus, who rescues us from the wrath to come.

In this passage, the apostle Paul provides important insights into the imminent nature of the rapture. Again, all four criteria are noted. First, Jesus will return at some unknown future time: "Jesus, who rescues us." Second, Paul implies Jesus will return quickly. He speaks as if Jesus could show up that day rather than some distant future time, though no specific time period is noted. Third, Christ's return is clearly something believers are to anticipate with joy. They are to "wait" for Him from heaven. They do not need to linger in fear, but rather, to serve the Lord in eager anticipation of His coming. Fourth, Christ's coming will be without judgment, especially since He will rescue us "from the wrath to come."

1 Thessalonians 5:4-9

> You, brethren, are not in darkness, that the day would overtake you like a thief; for you are all sons of light and sons of day. We are not of night nor of darkness; so then let us not sleep as others do, but let us be alert and sober. For those who sleep do their sleeping at night, and those who get drunk get drunk at night. But since we are of the day, let us be sober, having put on the breastplate of faith and love, and as a helmet, the hope of salvation. For God has not destined us for wrath, but for obtaining salvation through our Lord Jesus Christ…

Again, the apostle Paul addressed the coming of Christ in his first letter to the Thessalonian believers. The four criteria are noted, including Christ returning at any moment. First, the "day" will come quickly, like a "thief." Just as a thief arrives unexpectedly, so the rapture will take place at an unknown future time. Second, His coming is near. Paul specifically calls his readers to be "alert" because they do not know how soon Jesus might return. Third, His coming will provide salvation or rescue, and they were to anticipate His coming with joy. Fourth, His coming will offer salvation and escape from the coming wrath, "for God has not destined us for wrath."

1 Corinthians 1:7

> …so that you are not lacking in any gift, awaiting eagerly the revelation of our Lord Jesus Christ.

This brief passage again presents the apostle Paul writing to early believers regarding Christ's coming. First, he implies the rapture will take place at any moment rather than a specific time or in the distant future. Second, he teaches the Corinthian believers to eagerly await His "revelation," suggesting it could be near. No preceding signs were expected or required. Third, this revelation will be a positive event. They were to eagerly await His coming, when He would arrive as Lord. Fourth, no judgment is associated with this coming. This stands in contrast with the events connected with the second coming of Christ, when He will pour out judgment upon the earth (Revelation 19).

Titus 2:13

...looking for the blessed hope and the appearing of the glory of our great God and Savior, Christ Jesus.

Once again, Paul emphasizes key aspects of the rapture, as done in other passages. First, he appears to anticipate Jesus coming at any time. Second, he looks forward to the rapture taking place without expecting any additional events to occur beforehand. Third, the rapture is called "the blessed hope," clearly marking it as an encouraging event. Fourth, again there is no judgment associated with this event, which stands in stark contrast with the judgment that will take place at the second coming.

1 John 3:2-3

Beloved, now we are children of God, and it has not appeared as yet what we will be. We know that when He appears, we will be like Him, because we will see Him just as He is. And everyone who has this hope fixed on Him purifies himself, just as He is pure.

Up till now, we've seen imminency upheld in a direct quote from Jesus and four passages from the apostle Paul. Here, we come to the apostle John. First, the implication is that the rapture will take place any moment since "everyone who has this hope fixed on Him purifies himself." Second, no preceding signs are mentioned. John, one of the three apostles who were the closest to the Lord Jesus Christ, simply states, "When He appears…" Third, this coming rapture is clearly a time of hope and encouragement. Believers "will be like Him" and "will see Him just as He is." Fourth, no judgment is connected with this coming. Believers are given only positive statements about the future rapture event.

Revelation 22:7, 12, 20

> Behold, I am coming quickly. Blessed is he who heeds the words of the prophecy of this book…Behold, I am coming quickly, and My reward is with Me, to render to every man according to what he has done…He who testifies to these things says, "Yes, I am coming quickly." Amen. Come, Lord Jesus.

These three verses in Revelation 22 all highlight key aspects of the rapture—in what is the final chapter of Scripture. First, John makes it clear Jesus will come at any moment, for Jesus says, "I am coming quickly" three times. In this context, "the words of the prophecy of this book," or the events of Revelation, Christ speaks of His return as imminent. Second, though many signs are explained in the book of Revelation, none of them have to be fulfilled before Jesus comes. John simply writes, "Amen. Come, Lord Jesus." As Paul Feinberg notes, "There is no mention of any signs or events that precede the Rapture of the church in any of the Rapture passages. The point seems to be that the believer prior to this event is to look, not for some sign, but the Lord from heaven."[19] Third, the fact of Christ's imminent return brought great hope to John and was intended to encourage his readers. Fourth, though Revelation has much to say about God's judgments, these three verses about Jesus coming quickly anticipate only the positive aspects of what is to come—which supports the idea of the rapture taking place before the tribulation. Judgment is reserved only for those who will endure the tribulation and be present on the earth at the second coming.

Additional Biblical Support for Imminence

In addition to the seven aforementioned passages, there are six points we can observe in Scripture with regard to the timing of Christ's return at the rapture. These details further strengthen the case for Christ's at-any-moment return:

1. Future

The entire emphasis of the New Testament points to a future return of Christ. He promised, "I will come again" (John 14:3). The angels promised He would return (Acts 1:11). The apostles taught the certainty of His future return (Philippians 3:20; Titus 2:13; 2 Peter 3:3-8; 1 John 3:2-3).

2. Progressive

The present tense of "cometh" in 1 Thessalonians 5:2 (KJV) indicates that Jesus is in the process of coming again, marking the steady, uninterrupted movement of time toward that certain day. Hebrews 10:37 says, "For yet in a very little while, He who is coming will come, and will not delay."

3. Distant

From God's perspective, Jesus is coming at any moment. But from the human perspective, it has already been nearly 2,000 years. Jesus hinted at this in the Olivet Discourse when He spoke of the man who traveled into a "far country" (heaven—Matthew 25:14 KJV) and was gone "a long time" (verse 19). Peter also implies this in his prediction that, after the passing of a long period of time, people will scoff at the idea that Christ will ever return (2 Peter 3:4,8-9).

4. Undated

While the rapture is the next major event on the prophetic calendar, it is undated, as is the glorious appearing of Christ. Jesus said: "Of that day and hour knoweth no man, no, not the angels of heaven" (Matthew 24:36 KJV). Later he added: "It is not for you to know the times or the seasons" (Acts 1:7 KJV).

5. Unexpected

The global masses of humanity will not be looking for Christ when He returns (Matthew 24:50; Luke 21:35). They will be saying, "Peace and safety!" and will be caught unprepared by His coming (1 Thessalonians 5:3). So unexpected will be His return that "as a snare shall it come on all them that dwell on the face of the whole earth" (Luke 21:35 KJV).

6. Sudden

The Bible warns that Jesus will come "just like a thief in the night...then destruction will come upon them suddenly" (1 Thessalonians 5:2-3). Christ's return for His bride will occur in a flash: "in a moment, in the twinkling of an eye...for the trumpet will sound, and the dead [believers] will be raised imperishable, and we [living believers] will be changed" (1 Corinthians 15:52).[20]

Imminence Is the Only Reasonable Conclusion for the Rapture

We have defined imminence, responded to the arguments against the view that the rapture is imminent, and have examined seven specific Bible passages that affirm, in various ways, the imminent rapture of the church by Jesus Christ. Each passage either directly or indirectly points to the rapture taking place at any future moment, without any preceding signs. They also speak of the event as one that will bring encouragement to believers and is not associated with the judgments of the second coming. As Paul concludes in 1 Thessalonians 4:18, "Therefore comfort one another with these words."

Imminence Passages	
John 14:1-3	"I will come again and receive you to Myself"
1 Thessalonians 1:9-10	"Jesus…rescues us from the wrath to come"
1 Thessalonians 5:2	"[He comes] like a thief in the night"
1 Thessalonians 5:4-9	"Be sober…for God has not destined us for wrath"
1 Corinthians 1:7	"…awaiting eagerly the revelation of our Lord Jesus Christ"
Titus 2:13	"Looking for the blessed hope and the appearing of the glory of our great God and Savior, Christ Jesus"
1 John 3:2-3	"We know that when He appears, will will be like Him"
Revelation 22:7,12	"Behold, I am coming quickly"
Revelation 22:20	"Yes, I am coming quickly"

CHAPTER 9

Not Destined for Wrath

God has not destined us for wrath but for obtaining salvation through our Lord Jesus Christ.

1 THESSALONIANS 5:9

Scripture predicts the coming of a unique time of the outpouring of God's wrath in the end times. This time period is called by many names: the tribulation, the Great Tribulation, the Day of the Lord, the seventieth week, and the time of Jacob's trouble. Concerning the wrath of God during the Great Tribulation or the Day of the Lord, all the main views of the timing of the rapture, except the partial rapture view, agree that church-age believers are exempt from God's wrath.[1] All the views also agree that the protection from divine wrath during the Day of the Lord does not mean the church is exempt from all suffering, trials, persecution and trouble. Jesus told His followers, "In the world you have tribulation" (John 16:33). The apostle Paul warned us, "Through many tribulations we must enter the kingdom of God" (Acts 14:22). Many other passages reinforce this truth (John 15:18-20; 1 Thessalonians 3:3; 2 Timothy 3:12; 1 Peter 4:12-16).

There's a significant distinction in Scripture between tribulation in terms of trials and difficulties, and *the* tribulation, a time period during which God's wrath is poured out upon the earth. All believers face trials, troubles, and tribulations in daily life. By contrast, believers are specifically promised rescue from the outpouring of divine wrath in the Great Tribulation.

The issue at hand, then, is determining the time when the wrath of God begins and the means God uses to protect the church from it. Paul Feinberg notes, "It should be clear that the question of divine wrath is a fundamental one for the Rapture positions. The difference of opinion centers about the *commencement* of divine wrath and the *nature* of divine protection from that wrath."[2] Or to put it another way, how long will the wrath last, and how will God keep the church from that time?[3]

Here's how the four main views handle these issues.

Pretribulationists contend that the entire seven-year tribulation "is a time of divine wrath" and "the means of protection for the church is removal from this period by the Rapture."[4]

Midtribulationists believe the wrath during the first half of the final seven years is from man and Satan, while the wrath in the second half comes from God. The church will be raptured at the midpoint of the tribulation, before the wrath of God is expressed.

Prewrath rapturists hold that all the judgments before the sixth trumpet in Revelation 6 are human and satanic in origin, so the Day of the Lord (God's wrath) begins with the seventh trumpet. They locate the rapture about three-fourths of the way through the tribulation, between the sixth and seventh trumpets.

Posttribulationists maintain that the church will be on earth during the entire seven years of the tribulation but will be protected by God. The church won't be removed from the tribulation, but God will preserve the church in it.[5] The church won't be raptured until the time of the second advent. Another variation of this view contends God's wrath is concentrated right at the close of the tribulation, and the church will be raptured right before Armageddon at the very end.[6] Either way, posttribulationists believe the church is present on earth for the Great Tribulation.

The following chart shows how the different views of the rapture deal with the commencement of God's wrath and the nature of the deliverance from it.

	When the Wrath Commences	Nature of Divine Protection
Pretribulation	Beginning of the tribulation	Caught up to heaven
Midtribulation	Midpoint of the tribulation	Caught up to heaven
Posttribulation	The wrath of God is concentrated at the end of the tribulation	Protected on earth Caught up at the second coming
Prewrath	After the sixth trumpet	Caught up to heaven

Midtrib, prewrath, and posttrib proponents all believe the wrath of God begins at some point *after* the tribulation commences in Revelation 6:1 with the opening of the seals. They all see some part of the tribulation as the wrath of man and Satan, and not the wrath of God. They argue to varying degrees that war, famine, and disease are not the direct wrath of God. Paul Feinberg answers this argument well:

> To identify the wrath of God simply with His direct intervention is to overlook the fact that primary and secondary agency both belong to God. Would anyone deny that the Northern Kingdom had been judged by God because Assyria conquered her? Did the Southern Kingdom escape the wrath of God for her sin because the instrument of judgment was Nebuchadnezzar and Babylon? Surely the answer is no. Then why should anyone think that because the early seals and trumpets relate to famine and war as well as natural phenomena that they

cannot and are not expressions of the wrath of God?...
The incident in David's life where he numbered Israel
shows that God used Satan in bringing judgment
(2 Sam. 24:1; cf. 1 Chron. 21:10). The activity of the
whole period proceeds from the activity of the worthy
Lamb; it is He who breaks the seals.[7]

Furthermore, famine, war, and plagues are often associated with
God's wrath in other places in the Bible (Jeremiah 14:12; 15:2; 24:10;
29:17; Ezekiel 5:12, 17; 14:21). The nature of the entire tribulation
period demands that Christ's bride be exempt from all of it, not
just part.

It's All God's Wrath

All three series judgments in Revelation 6–18 (seals, trumpets,
and bowls) are manifestations of God's wrath.[8] The seal judgments,
which take place at the very beginning of the tribulation, are initi-
ated when Jesus breaks the first of the seven seals (Revelation 6:1).
To suggest that the wrath of God is somehow limited to the last half,
last one-fourth, or very end of the tribulation ignores the source of
the seven seal judgments that commence the seven-year tribulation.

We believe the judgments of the *entire* seven-year tribulation
period are a manifestation of God's wrath unleashed against a defi-
ant world. The judgment of God begins with the first seal that is
opened in Revelation 6:1 and continues all the way until the second coming in Revelation 19:11-21. There are at least seven clear references in the book of Revelation to God's wrath (6:17-18; 14:8-10;
14:19; 15:7; 16:1, 19; 19:15).

Sometimes those who hold to the pretrib view are accused of
being escapists who are unwilling to suffer for their faith. Yet, as
we've said, all the views believe Christians will be exempt from God's
wrath. Moreover, for a believer to desire to escape God's wrath during the tribulation is not sub-Christian. As John Walvoord says: "Is

it an unworthy motive to desire to escape the Great Tribulation? Actually it is no more so than the desire to escape hell. The point in either case is not our desire or wishes but the question as to what the Scriptures promise. Pretribulationists hope to escape the Great Tribulation because it is expressly a time of divine judgment on a world that has rejected Christ."[9]

Exempt from God's Wrath

We're forced to ask this signficant question: Why would God leave His bride on earth during this time? It makes no sense. What purpose does it serve for Jesus to batter and brutalize His bride before He comes to rescue her? As J.F. Strombeck says, "One is forced to ask, how could the Lamb of God die and rise again to save the Church from wrath and then allow her to pass through the wrath that He shall pour upon those who reject Him? Such inconsistency might be possible in the thinking of men, but not in the acts of the Son of God."[10]

While the future rapture is not mentioned in the Old Testament, we see from examples in the biblical text that it is generally against God's nature and purposes to judge the righteous alongside the wicked when He deliberately pours out divine wrath as a judgment against human rejection and disobedience. While there are exceptions, like believers carried into captivity along with unbelievers, the believers' suffering was a result of corporate judgment on the nation as a whole.

The Bible clearly promises, in at least three places, that God's people in this age are exempt from the wrath to come during the tribulation period: 1 Thessalonians 1:9-10; 5:9, and Revelation 3:10. Let's examine each of the passages in their context and let Scripture speak for itself.

1 Thessalonians 1:9-10

In these verses, Paul reminds the believers at Thessalonica of how they readily turned from dead idols to the living God, and comments on how they are waiting for the coming of Jesus from heaven. Exemption from eschatological wrath of the tribulation is explicitly promised: "They themselves report about us what kind of a reception we had with you, and how you turned to God from idols to serve a living and true God, and to wait for His Son from heaven, whom He raised from the dead, that is Jesus, who *rescues us from the wrath to come*" (emphasis added).

There are three uses of the Greek preposition *ek* ("from," "out of") in 1:10. Without some clear indication in the text, consistency demands that all three uses carry the same meaning. The believers were waiting for Jesus to come from (*ek*) heaven, the one who was raised "from [*ek*] the dead." This same person would deliver the believers "from [*ek*] the wrath to come." The first two uses of *ek* clearly mean "from" or "out of." Jesus will come *out of* heaven and was raised *out from* the dead, so it makes sense that the final use of *ek*, in reference to God's wrath, must have the same connotation. The preposition *ek* "emphasizes the completeness of our rescue by Christ—we are rescued out of the time of distress itself."[11]

The word "delivers" (Greek, *rhuomai*) is a strong word that carries the meaning of rescuing from something by a forcible act.[12] The word "places the emphasis on the greatness of the peril from which deliverance is given by a mighty act of power."[13] The word "delivers" is a present-tense participle which stresses that the church's "deliverance or separation from the future wrath was already a present reality when Paul wrote in 1 Thessalonians 1:10."[14] Because our deliverance or separation from wrath is already a present reality, we can rest assured that we will be separated from the wrath of the Day of the Lord.

The next question is, What particular wrath is in view? The word "wrath" (Greek, *orge*) has a definite article in front of it, so it's not referring to just any wrath, but *the* wrath to come. Some view this as eternal wrath in hell because in the previous verses in 1 Thessalonians, Paul talked about election and salvation, not eschatology.[15] Of course, all agree that believers are protected from this aspect of God's wrath; however, in the context of 1 Thessalonians, which contains frequent reference to the Lord's coming, the wrath in 1:10 points to eschatological wrath (cf. 1 Thessalonians 5:1-9).[16] Also, the verse says that believers will be delivered from this wrath by the Lord's coming. His coming is not what delivers believers from the wrath of hell; rather, it will deliver them from the wrath of the Day of the Lord.

Posttrib proponents argue that God's people are on earth during the tribulation "but not as the recipients of God's wrath."[17] In other words, believers will be present during the time, but will not experience the wrath. But this view fails to give full force to the word *ek* in the context of 1 Thessalonians, and the fact that the means of deliverance from this wrath is the coming of Jesus. It's the coming of the Son from heaven that delivers us from the wrath. The only logical way His coming from heaven can deliver us *from* the wrath is if He *removes* us from it. This strongly supports the pretrib position. So, to summarize, this verse teaches us:

- Believers will be kept from or out of the eschatological wrath of God.

- The means of deliverance from that wrath is the coming of Jesus.

1 Thessalonians 5:1-9

This passage supports the pretrib view in three ways. First, this passage comes right on the heels of the classic rapture text in 1 Thessalonians 4:13-18. The sequence or chronology of these two passages is instructive. First Thessalonians 4:13-18 deals with the resurrection of dead believers and the rapture of living saints to meet the Lord in the air at His coming. This is followed in 1 Thessalonians 5:1 by the introduction of a new topic. The transition is marked by the words, "Now as to" (Greek, *peri de*), which signals a change of subject (see as done by Paul elsewhere—1 Corinthians 7:1, 25; 8:1; 12:1; 16:1, 12; 1 Thessalonians 4:9):

> Now as to the times and the epochs, brethren, you have no need of anything to be written to you. For you yourselves know full well that the day of the Lord will come just like a thief in the night (1 Thessalonians 5:1-2).

The introduction of a new, but related, subject is significant because of the order of the events. The rapture is described in 1 Thessalonians 4:13-18, and then the Day of the Lord or tribulation is discussed in 1 Thessalonians 5:1-9. This sequence indicates the rapture is followed by the Day of the Lord. They're sequential, not simultaneous. The rapture must come before the Day of the Lord, not consummate it. The rapture and the Day of the Lord can hardly be parts of the same event, as posttribulationists maintain.[18] The same can be said of so-called historic (or general) premillennialists, who do not see a specific seven-year Tribulation, but do hold to both the rapture and the return occurring simultaneously before a literal 1,000-year millennium.

The difference between 1 Thessalonians 4:13-18 and 1 Thessalonians 5:1-9 is further highlighted by the fact that the believers were "uninformed" concerning the truth of the rapture in 4:13, while in 5:1 they were well aware of the truth regarding the Day of the Lord. These are two separate but related topics.

Another point in 1 Thessalonians 5:1-3 that supports the pretrib position is the interplay between two different audiences, as evidenced by the shift in pronouns. Notice the italicized words in this passage:

> Now as to the times and the epochs, brethren, *you* have no need of anything to be written to *you*. For *you yourselves* know full well that the day of the Lord will come

just like a thief in the night. While *they* are saying, "Peace and safety!" then destruction will come upon *them* suddenly like birth pangs upon a woman with child; and *they* will not escape. But *you*, brethren, are not in darkness, that the day should overtake *you* like a thief; for *you* are all sons of light and sons of the day. *We* are not of night nor of darkness (emphasis added).

The sudden shift between *you* and *we* (believers) in the first and second person, and *they* and *them* (unbelievers) in the third person, is striking. The change of pronouns indicates that when the tribulation arrives, there will be two distinct groups of people. One group, the saved, will be rescued. And the other, the unsaved, will face divine retribution.

Notice, the Day of the Lord will come upon *them*, and *they* will not escape (5:3). Unbelievers will find themselves in the crosshairs of God's retribution. Then, in verse 4, there's a sudden contrast: "But *you*, brethren, are not in darkness." *They* stands in sharp contrast to the believers ("you") who will escape (5:4-11). This clear differentiation between the unbelievers, who will not escape the Day of the Lord, and the believers, who will escape, is another argument that believers are exempt from the wrath of the Day of the Lord.

Third, in 1 Thessalonians 5:9 we read, "God has not destined us for wrath, but for obtaining salvation through our Lord Jesus Christ." This verse tells us that believers have an appointment with salvation, not wrath. Many commentators believe the "wrath" in this verse refers to the wrath of hell, from which believers will be spared. Yet the entire context of 1 Thessalonians 5:1-8 is Day of the Lord wrath, not eternal wrath in hell. The wrath is the anguish and tribulation associated from the beginning of the Day of the Lord (see v. 3), and it is from this that the believer has been delivered by the one who "delivers us from the wrath to come."[19] Believers are promised "exemption for the entirety of the future horrors of the earthly tribulation period."[20]

Believers are appointed for salvation or deliverance, not the wrath of the Day of the Lord.

Dr. John Walvoord puts it simply: "In this passage he is expressly saying that our appointment is to be caught up to be with Christ; the appointment of the world is for the Day of the Lord, the day of wrath. One cannot keep both of these appointments."[21] We make our appointment for salvation and rescue when we trust Jesus Christ as our personal Savior from sin—the one who bore our judgment and God's wrath on the cross.

Revelation 3:10

In Revelation 3:10, Jesus makes this promise to the church at Philadelphia: "Because you have kept the word of My perseverance, I also will keep you from the hour of testing, that hour which is about to come upon the whole world, to test those who dwell on the earth."

The meaning of the phrase "I also will keep you from the hour of testing" has engendered much discussion and debate about the timing of the rapture. With regard to Revelation 3:10, Bible interpreters fall into three main camps:

1. The promise is limited to the church of Philadelphia and has no larger scope or application. This view is refuted by Jesus's statement that His message is for all the churches (verse 13). Also, the scope of this passage is global, involving "the whole world."

2. Believers are assured they will be preserved through the time of tribulation.

3. The passage promises that no believer will be present for any of the future tribulation.

Four key factors point to view three as the best interpretation.

THE PREPOSITION

The main debate over how to understand Revelation 3:10 revolves around whether the Greek words *tereo ek* ("keep from") mean "protect from or through," or "remove from." A great deal of ink has been spilled over the meaning of the preposition *ek* in this verse. Pretribulationists argue that *tereo ek* supports the notion of evacuation from the earth before the tribulation. Posttribulationists argue that *ek* in this verse means "through"—that is, protection from the wrath *while* on earth during the tribulation. They state that the Lord will keep and preserve believers "from" or "through" the wrath of God, not "out of" the time of it.

The only other use of *tereo ek* in the New Testament is in John 17:15, which says, "I do not ask You to take them out of the world, but to *keep* them *from* the evil one" (emphasis added). The usage of this identical phrase in John 17:15 supports the meaning of *ek* in Revelation 3:10 as "to keep from completely" or "out from within."[22] God doesn't keep His people *through* Satan—the evil one; He keeps us *from* him (1 John 5:18). "Since John 17:15 means 'to keep outside' of the evil one, then the parallel thought in Revelation 3:10 is to keep the church outside the hour of testing. Therefore, only a pretribulation rapture would fulfill the promise."[23]

A simpler argument is that if the Lord had meant that believers would be kept "through" the tribulation, there are far better ways to have expressed this. Charles Ryrie says,

> If, as postribs say, the promise is that the church will live through the Tribulation under divine protection and emerge at the end, then why was a different preposition not used which would convey that meaning? For instance, "in" (*en*) would mean the church would be kept (safely) in that time. Or why not "through" (*dia*) which would mean kept through the Tribulation? Why "from" (*ek*)? Because that means the church will be removed from the time, and that means a pretrib rapture.[24]

Getting straight to the point, the idea of keeping or removing believers from the tribulation "is the most natural and simplest translation of the word *ek*."[25]

If, as posttribulationists say, Revelation 3:10 is a promise of protection and preservation for believers *through* the tribulation, then how does one explain the massive casualty count of believers in Revelation 6–18?[26] (see Revelation 7:13-14; 13:10, 15; 20:4). As Andy Woods says,

> If this is a divine promise, then God does a poor job keeping it since Revelation also records the numerous martyrdoms of believers during the tribulation period... Thus, it is inaccurate to suggest that if the church is on the earth during the tribulation period, it will enjoy divine protection. If this were so, then the countless martyrdoms during this time period are inexplicable.[27]

It is true that Revelation 9:4 and 16:2 mention divine protection of believers on earth from the fifth trumpet and first bowl judgments, but these are the only two references to God sparing believers on earth during the tribulation. (These believers on earth are not part of the church, but people who received salvation in Christ after the rapture. We often call them "tribulation saints.") With the exception of the judgments in Revelation 9:4 and 16:2, all the seal, trumpet, and bowl judgments will be experienced by believers and unbelievers alike. Beginning in Revelation 6, divine wrath will be falling everywhere. There will be no place on earth to hide. The global scope of the wrath makes it difficult to see how preservation could be achieved by any means other than removal via the rapture.[28]

Finally, Jesus gave this promise in Revelation 3:10 to comfort the beleaguered church at Philadelphia. If believers will be present on earth during this time of global upheaval, persecution, and massive martyrdom, how comforting would Jesus's words really be? Would they serve as any real source of consolation or encouragement?[29]

THE PERIOD

Jesus promised to keep His people not just from, or out of, the testing of the tribulation, but from the "hour" or time of testing. The church's exemption is not just from the testing of the Great Tribulation, but from the very time of the testing, which indicates we will be spared from the time of tribulation itself. The assurance of protection from the time of the testing adds further support to the pretrib notion of *removal* out of the tribulation, not the posttrib idea of *safeguarding* or *protection* through it.

> Christ promised to keep these church saints from the time period characterized by the testing Christ has in mind. If the Lord had meant that He would keep them from just the testing itself, He could have made that very clear by omitting the words "the hour" and simply saying, "I will keep you from the testing" …If people live within a time period, they are not separated from it… The only way to keep people from an entire time period is to prevent them from entering it.[30]

Jesus was clear: "I…will keep you from the *hour* of testing" (emphasis added). As Norman Geisler says, "One cannot be saved from an entire hour by being any part of it."[31] Stripping away all the details, and "the most natural reading of 'kept from the hour' is not to be present through it, but to be kept safe in a place away from where it occurs."[32]

THE PURPOSE

In Revelation 3:10, Jesus said the purpose of the coming global judgment is "to test those who dwell on the earth." These "earth dwellers," referred to for the first time in 3:10, are referred to ten more times in the book of Revelation. Throughout Revelation they are recognized as enemies of God, persecutors of God's people, and objects of God's wrath because of their hardened, incorrigible rebellion against the Lord. According to Jesus, one of the primary purposes of the future time of worldwide testing is to try these unbelieving earth dwellers. The purpose of this period is not to test or try believers, but the wicked. They're the special objects of this judgment. Why would the church need to be present during this time of universal judgment specifically designed for the wicked earth dwellers? It makes no sense for Christians to be present during that time. And we won't be. The Lord has promised He will spare the church from the tribulation.

The Promise

Immediately on the heels of reassuring believers that He would remove them from the future time of worldwide testing, Jesus promised them, "I am coming quickly" (Revelation 3:11). The placement of this statement immediately after the promise of deliverance from the time of testing indicates that the coming of Jesus is the means God will use to bring about the church's removal. This sequence strongly implies that the deliverance of Christians from the hour of testing will occur in conjunction with Christ's coming.[33] This promise of Jesus, then, is consistent with the pretrib rapture view.

The Summary

Taking into account all the parts of Revelation 3:10-11, we see that Jesus will protect His church *from* the *time* of *worldwide* testing *by* His coming for them at the rapture. Paul Benware summarizes it this way: "The promise is to keep the church from the time period of testing, which necessitates actual removal from the time period itself and not preservation through it. The means of the removal from the universal time period of testing is the Rapture prior to the beginning of the Tribulation."[34]

Whatever view one takes of Revelation 3:10, it must harmonize well with the rest of the book of Revelation. It's never proper to wrench a text out of its larger context. The pretrib rapture view of Revelation 3:10 meets this criterion of contextual consistency. The word "church" (Greek, *ekklesia*) is found 20 times in Revelation. It's used 19 times in chapters 1–3, then the word doesn't appear again until Revelation 22:16. After Revelation 3, the next time we meet the bride of Christ, she's in heaven with Jesus, preparing to return with Him to earth (Revelation 19:7-8). The absence of the church on earth from Revelation 4 to Revelation 18 is consistent with the pretrib view of Revelation 3:10.

Theologian Charles Ryrie provides a helpful illustration of the timing of the rapture in relation to the testing mentioned in Revelation 3:10:

> As a teacher I frequently give exams. Let's suppose that I announce an exam will occur on such and such a day at the regular class time. Then suppose I say, "I want to make a promise to students whose grade average for the semester so far is A. The promise is: I will keep you from the exam."
>
> Now I could keep my promise to those A students this way: I would tell them to come to the exam, pass out the exam to everyone, and give the A students a sheet containing the answers. They would take the exam and yet in reality be kept from the exam. They would live through the time but not suffer the trial. This is posttribulationism: protection while enduring.
>
> But if I said to the class, "I am giving an exam next week. I want to make a promise to all the A students. I

will keep you from the hour of the exam." They would understand clearly that to be kept from the hour of the test exempts them from being present during that hour. This is pretribulationism, and this is the meaning of the promise of Revelation 3:10. And the promise came from the risen Savior who Himself is the deliverer of the wrath to come (1 Thessalonians 1:10).[35]

The Assurance of Exemption

Both the apostle Paul and Jesus promised Christians exemption from the time period during which God would pour out His wrath on the earth. The best way to explain these assurances in their respective scriptural contexts is to hold to the view that believers will be removed from the earth before the outbreak of the global conflagration.

CHAPTER 10

The Necessity of an Interval Between the Rapture and the Return

*A careful study of related Scripture will demonstrate
that an interval of time between the translation of
the church and the coming of Christ to establish
the millennial kingdom is absolutely necessary.*[1]

JOHN F. WALVOORD

Among the arguments in support of the pretribulation rapture, one strong proof that is often ignored or unnoticed is the necessity of a time interval or gap between the rapture and the return of Jesus Christ. This interlude of time is required in order for four events to occur that Scripture places after the rapture but before the return. The pretrib rapture provides the required time for these four events to transpire (as do the midtrib and prewrath views), but that's not the case for the posttrib position.[2] Two of these events occur in heaven during the tribulation, and two of them take place on earth.

Four Events that Must Occur
The Judgment Seat (Bema) *of Christ*
Second Corinthians 5:10 says that all Christians must appear before the judgment seat of Christ in heaven to be reviewed and rewarded for their service to the Lord. This event is never referenced in the detailed accounts connected with the second coming of Christ to the earth. There is biblical evidence, however, that

the judgment seat will occur after the rapture and *before* the second coming.

For example, 1 Corinthians 4:5 says, "Do not go on passing judgment before the time, but wait until the Lord comes who will both bring to light the things hidden in the darkness and disclose the motives of men's hearts; and then each man's praise will come to him from God." The evaluation of believers will occur when the Lord comes. This evaluation will apparently require some time to carry out, and that will be made possible by the pretrib view's gap of seven years between the rapture and the second coming.

Revelation 19:7-10 provides further support that the judgment seat of Christ will occur between the rapture and the return. Paul Benware summarizes this argument well:

> This event apparently takes place in connection with the Rapture but prior to the Second Coming because, at the Second Coming, these believers have already been rewarded. The church has been rewarded in Revelation 19:8, where John states that "it was given to her [the church] to clothe herself in fine linen, bright and clean; for the fine linen is the righteous acts of the saints." The garments represent the rewards. The fact that the Bride is wearing her beautiful garments indicates that she has already received her rewards for her deeds of righteousness. The time of this event is clearly right before the Lord Jesus descends from heaven to conquer the world as King of kings and Lord of lords. The judgment seat of Christ, therefore, must take place prior to the Second Coming but after the church is taken to heaven by the Lord Jesus. This rewarding of believers assumes that some length of time must be involved. And a rapture that occurs before the final seven years allows for that needed time.[3]

Because the rewarded bride will accompany Jesus back to earth at His return (Revelation 19:14), it is necessary for her to have gone up to heaven some time previously. The presence of the rewarded bride in heaven prior to the second coming and her return with Jesus to earth is a difficult hurdle for posttribulationists to overcome.[4]

Nevertheless, George Eldon Ladd, a posttrib advocate, questions whether seven years between the rapture and the return is enough time for the judgment seat to take place. He says,

> It is estimated that there are two hundred million living Christians [this was written in 1956]. In seven years, there are just over two hundred million seconds. How much of a fraction of a second is necessary for the judgment of each believer? If an interval of time is needed, then far more than seven years will be required.[5]

We have no way of knowing how the Lord will judge every believer in the span of seven years, but we can rest assured that it poses no obstacle for an unlimited God who is all-powerful and all-knowing. As John Walvoord observes, "We can infer from such judgments as that of the sheep and the goats (Matt. 25:31-46) that there is no divine problem in judging millions at once. Undoubtedly, only a fraction of the seven years between the Rapture and the Lord's return to the earth is occupied with judgments."[6]

While God's ways in carrying out this judgment, or any of the other judgments, may be beyond our ability to comprehend, what we can say with certainty is that Scripture indicates this judgment will happen before the second coming—which, in turn, supports a pretribulation timing for the rapture.

The Marriage of the Lamb

Revelation 19:7-8 describes an event in heaven known as "the marriage of the Lamb." This will immediately precede the second coming of Christ to earth: "Let us rejoice and be glad and give the glory to Him, for the marriage of the Lamb has come and His bride has made herself ready. It was given to her to clothe herself in fine linen, bright and clean; for the fine linen is the righteous acts of the saints."

A few verses later, in Revelation 19:14, the same bride, clothed in fine linen, returns with Jesus to earth at His second advent.

Note that the presentation of the bride to Jesus does not occur in the clouds or on earth, but in heaven. It will be accompanied by great joy. This event will require a time interval between the rapture and return so that the bride can be in heaven for the marriage and being clothed in fine garments before returning with Christ to earth. This supports the pretrib view and poses a problem for posttribulationism.

One posttribulational counter to this point is that the marriage of the Lamb could occur in a brief moment of time, making a lengthy interval between the rapture and the return unnecessary. However, this argument contradicts the posttribulational argument that the judgment seat of Christ would require more than seven years. When it comes to events that take place after the rapture and before the second coming, you can't suggest one event will occur in a moment and then argue that another event would require more than seven years.

Another answer posttribulationalists give is that the marriage of the Lamb in Revelation 19 is a vision and simply a prophetic hymn or announcement of what will happen later. In other words, the marriage of the Lamb doesn't happen in heaven before the second coming in Revelation 19, but is simply announced at that time. Posttribulationists believe the actual marriage will occur in Revelation 20 in the millennial kingdom.[7] To support this view, they point to the verse that precedes the description of the marriage of the Lamb, which says, "Hallelujah! For the Lord our God, the Almighty, reigns" (Revelation 19:6). Since this verse is proleptic and looks ahead to the millennial kingdom, they contend that the marriage of the Lamb should also be moved to that setting.

While this perspective certainly helps posttribulationists, it's important to note that Revelation 19:7 says, "The marriage of the Lamb has come and the bride has made herself ready." The phrase "has come" points to a *present* setting in the context before the second coming. Also, at the marriage, the bride is clothed in fine linen (verse 8), and that same clothing is worn by those who accompany Jesus during His return from heaven (verse 14). This reveals a sequential progression in Revelation 19, where the bride, dressed in fine linen, is joined to Christ in heaven at the marriage and then returns with Him to earth. The repetition of the words, "And I saw" (Greek, *kai eidon*) in Revelation 19–21 indicates that John is seeing events in a sequential, chronological order (Revelation 19:11, 17, 19; 20:1, 4, 11; 21:1). He is seeing one thing followed by another, followed by another, etc.

The marriage of the Lamb to the bride in heaven before the second coming supports the pretrib view and represents an impediment to the posttrib position.

The Judgment of the Sheep and the Goats

In some of His final words on earth, Jesus prophesied His own return to judge living Gentiles who survive the time of global tribulation. He pictured Himself as a Shepherd separating sheep (believers) from goats (unbelievers): "When the Son of Man comes in His glory, and all the angels with Him, then He will sit on His glorious throne. All the nations will be gathered before Him; and He will separate them from one another, as the shepherd separates the sheep from the goats; and He will put the sheep on His right, and the goats on the left" (Matthew 25:31-33). This passage refers to the judgment of the nations.

From the setting in Matthew 25, we know that those assembled at this judgment will be Gentile survivors of the Great Tribulation.

When Jesus comes back, these people will be gathered before the returning King. At this judgment, Jesus will divide these Gentiles into two categories—the sheep (believers) and the goats (unbelievers). This clearly reveals that when Jesus returns at His second coming, there will be both unbelievers and believers alive on the earth. Why is this significant for the timing of the rapture?

The issue here is simple. If the rapture and the return occur simultaneously, as posttribulationists believe, and every living believer is raptured to meet Jesus as He descends to earth, then who are the sheep on earth when Jesus arrives? The only people who will be left on earth would be the goats. There wouldn't be any sheep—they would have all just been raptured. Obviously, "there is no way the rapture can remove the sheep yet have them present on the earth immediately following the rapture to be judged."[8]

John MacArthur and Richard Mayhue suggest, "If the rapture occurs in connection with a posttribulational coming, the subsequent separation of the sheep from the goats in Matthew 25:31-46 would be redundant."[9] To state this another way, the saved and unsaved, still in their natural bodies, cannot be separated on earth immediately after the second coming if all living believers have already been caught up before immediately turning around and coming back. There would be no need to separate the sheep from the goats because the rapture would have already accomplished that task.

Only a pretribulational rapture would allow time for many people on the earth to become saved during the tribulation. These tribulation saints, then, would be the sheep of Matthew 25:31-46 when Jesus returns. This makes the judgment of the nations one of the most compelling arguments against posttribulationism.

Interestingly, most posttribulational commentators don't even attempt to answer this question. They seem to just ignore it. One could speculate about the reason for their silence, but clearly at least one reason is that there is no easy answer to this problem within their view.

To his credit, Robert Gundry, a posttribulationist, has attempted to take on this issue. Gundry's main solution is to move the judgment of the nations in Matthew 25:31-46 from the time of the second coming to the end of the millennium. By moving this event, he gets around the issue of all the sheep being raptured to heaven at the second coming with no sheep left on earth.[10] Gundry relocates the judgment in Matthew 25 to the end of the millennium. He equates the judgment of the sheep and the goats in Matthew 25:31-46 with the Great White Throne judgment in Revelation 20:11-15.[11]

The major obstacle Gundry faces is that there are substantial differences evident between these two judgments when we place them side-by-side.

Sheep and Goats	Great White Throne[12]
No resurrection	Resurrection of the dead
No books opened	Books opened
The word *nations* used	The word *dead* used
Sheep (believers) present	No mention of believers
Three groups mentioned: sheep, goats, brethren	Only one group mentioned: the dead
Reward is the kingdom and eternal life	No mention of reward, only condemnation
Occurs at the place Christ comes (the earth)	Earth has fled away

Another problem with Gundry's placement of the sheep and goats judgment at the end of the millennium is that the entire setting of Matthew 24–25 is the second coming of Christ and the days of tribulation that immediately precede it. Matthew 24:29-30 identifies the glorious appearing of Christ as "after the tribulation" of those days.[13] Christ's coming in glory with His angels in Matthew 25:31 is consistent with 2 Thessalonians 1:7, which describes the second coming. Matthew 25:31 bears semblance to Zechariah 14:5 and Daniel 7:13-14, which are also passages about Christ's second coming.[14]

Matthew 25:31-46 remains a major, stubborn obstacle for the posttribulation view. The answers posttribulationists have provided thus far are not convincing to most objective interpreters of Scripture. If Matthew 25:31 refers to the second coming, then posttribulationism is, at a minimum, soundly refuted, and one could even argue it rendered impossible—whereas pretribulationism remains a viable option.

Populating the Kingdom

A final compelling argument for the necessity of a time gap between the rapture and the return involves the people who are needed to help populate the messianic kingdom.[15] For those who believe in a literal, earthly messianic kingdom after Christ's return to earth, it's necessary to have people enter that kingdom in non-glorified human bodies, for only they will be able to bear children and populate the kingdom. This is not an issue for amillennialists or postmillennialmists, who reject the notion of a literal, 1,000-year reign of Christ after He returns.

The problem arises from the fact that the Bible teaches that when Christ returns to earth, Old Testament saints, church-age believers, and believers who died during the tribulation will all enter the millennial kingdom in new, glorified bodies. But believers who come to faith in Christ during the tribulation and live until the second advent will enter the millennial kingdom of Christ in their natural, human bodies. During the messianic reign, it is they who will serve as farmers and build houses. And they will also bear children, which will help populate our Lord's kingdom (Isaiah 65:20-25).

With these thoughts in mind, here's the issue in a nutshell. It would be impossible for people to enter the 1,000-year reign of Christ in natural bodies if all saints were caught up at the Second

Coming and glorified, as posttribulationists teach. Why? Because every believer would already have a glorified body. There wouldn't be anyone left in natural bodies to populate the kingdom.

Dr. John Walvoord captures the essence of this problem for posttribulationists and offers a solid solution.

> Certain problems immediately arise if the church is not translated until the end of the Tribulation. Nothing is more evident in the passage dealing with the translation of the church than the fact that every believer on that occasion is translated, that is, transformed from a body of flesh to an immortal body and caught up from the earth…If the translation takes place *after* the Tribulation, the question facing the posttribulationists is a very obvious one. Who is going to populate the earth during the Millennium? The Scriptures are specific that during the Millennium saints will build houses and bear children and have normal, mortal lives on earth. If all believers are translated and all unbelievers are put to death at the beginning of the Millennium, there will be no one left to populate the earth and fulfill these Scriptures…The best answer to our problem of who will populate the millennial earth is an obvious one. If the church is translated before the tribulation period, there is ample time for a new generation of believers to come into being from Jewish and Gentile background to qualify for entrance into the millennial kingdom at the second coming of Christ.[16]

Charles Ryrie highlights the problem the posttribulation view has with populating the kingdom:

> So, either the posttribulationist must find some people who will not be saved when the rapture begins but who will be saved at the instantaneous rapture/second

coming event; or, he must allow the initial parents in the Millennium to be unsaved people who somehow are not killed or judged at or after Armageddon. Those are the only options by which the posttribulationist can find millennial parents.[17]

Most posttribulationists do not attempt to answer this question, but the issue remains a stubborn problem for their view.[18] Robert Gundry proposes a unique solution. Based on Zechariah 14:16, he argues that unredeemed survivors of the tribulation will enter the millennial kingdom of Christ. This solves the problem of not having believers in glorified bodies to populate the kingdom.

What does Zechariah 14:16 say? Let's take a closer look: "It will come about that any who are left of all the nations that went against Jerusalem will go up from year to year to worship the King, the LORD of hosts, and to celebrate the Feast of Booths."

Next, here is Gundry's explanation of his view:

> That those who enter the millennium will include wicked survivors of the tribulation derives from the phraseology—"*everyone* who is left of *all* the nations." It also derives from the inclusion of those who attacked Jerusalem—i.e., the armies of the wicked who will converge on Palestine at the close of the tribulation—and form the implication that some of those who will enter the millennium will refuse to go to Jerusalem for the worship of the Lord, a refusal hardly characteristic of the righteous. This passage, therefore, goes against any interpretation which would prohibit the wicked from entering the millennium.[19]

Gundry's view, however, makes Zechariah 14:16 say more than the text actually states. The passage does *not* prove that unsaved people will enter the millennium. In the context of Zechariah 14, those who are left from the nations that went up against Jerusalem are saved people from those nations which participated in Armageddon. Not *all* the people from every nation who go up against Jerusalem will be unbelievers. Zechariah 14:16 actually speaks of believers who originated from those rebellious nations and were brought into the kingdom.

It's important to note that, according to Matthew 24:37-41, unbelievers will *not* enter the kingdom:

> The coming of the Son of Man will be just like the days of Noah. For as in those days before the flood they were eating and drinking, marrying and giving in marriage, until the day that Noah entered the ark, and they did not understand until the flood came and took them all away; so will the coming of the Son of Man be. Then there will be two men in the field; one will be taken and one will be left. Two women will be grinding at the mill; one will be taken and one will be left.

Those taken away at the time of Jesus's return will be carried off to judgment, just as in the days of Noah. As Ryrie points out, "The posttribulationist must add the stipulation that not all who are left are judged and condemned, so that there will be some left to populate the earth."[20] Yet Scripture says *all* unbelievers will be taken away to judgment when Jesus comes. None will be left to enter the kingdom. Matthew 13:40-42 states it plainly:

> Just as the tares are gathered up and burned with fire, so shall it be at the end of the age. The Son of Man will send forth His angels, and they will gather out of His kingdom all stumbling blocks, and those who commit lawlessness, and will throw them into the furnace of fire; in that place there will be weeping and gnashing of teeth.

The tares, which picture the unredeemed, are gathered "out of His kingdom."

The posttribulational search for unredeemed people to populate the kingdom goes against the clear teaching of Jesus in Matthew 13 and 24. If their view leaves no redeemed people in mortal bodies to enter the kingdom, and Scripture eliminates all unredeemed from entering the kingdom, then posttribulationism comes to an immovable roadblock, rendering it incompatible with premillennialism.[21]

The issue of how the kingdom will become populated does not prove the pretribulation view, but it is consistent with it. Pretribulationism has at least a seven-year interval between the removal of the church at the rapture and the return of Christ to the earth, which means finding parents to populate the millennial kingdom is not a problem. Millions of people on earth will be saved during the interval between the rapture and the return. Many of them will be martyred for their faith, but some will survive and enter the millennium in their natural bodies. This means they will be able to bear children, and as Scripture says, some of these children will eventually go on to reject Christ.

What the Interval Means

When the events of the end times are arranged in an orderly, systematic pattern, the necessity of a time interval between the rapture and the return becomes apparent. This time interval requirement causes major problems for posttribulationists, but not pretribulationists. This provides yet another strand in the theological cable that supports the prettribulationist view.

CHAPTER 11

Does It Really Matter?

A gloomy pessimistic unrealized eschatology
that thinks we can't make a difference in
the world as the church by the power of
the gospel is...an extreme error.[1]

GERRY BRESHEARS AND MARK DRISCOLL

What we believe about God and His involvement in the world really does matter. In that regard, what we believe about the Bible matters because truth matters.[2] Every theological system results in issues of practical application. How we apply what we believe to the world in which we live is a direct result of our biblical and theological perspective. In other words, what we believe about a particular matter (for example, the pretribulational rapture) does have consequences for how we view the church's responsibility to proclaim the gospel to the world.

The practical application of any eschatology must answer four basic questions:

1. What can we affirm?
2. How does it work?
3. Where does it lead?
4. Why does it matter?

For example, if one's eschatology affirms that we are already in the millennium, his or her view will tend to emphasize the idea that the millennial promises are spiritual rather than literal, and that they will be fulfilled by the church rather than by Israel. By contrast, those who believe the millennial promises will be fulfilled literally tend to view the millennium as a literal period of 1,000 years, during which Christ will reign on the earth. Thus, each eschatological view will answer the four questions differently.

Premillennialists believe Christ must return *before* there will ever be millennial conditions on the earth. Therefore, we view satanic opposition as a present reality because we believe Satan is not yet bound in the sense that Revelation 20:1-3 predicts he will be during the millennium.[3] By contrast, most amillennial and postmillennial interpreters view Satan as already bound either from preventing the spread of the gospel or from hindering its application to the elect.[4] For them, Christ will return *after* the church succeeds in bringing in millennial conditions on the earth (either spiritually or literally).

Glenn Kreider rightly suggests that all Christian eschatology is optimistic because it is a "message of hope that one day God will complete his work of redemption."[5] In other words, we all believe that God will triumph in the end. The differences of application come as a result of when and how we believe God's work will be accomplished. While we may differ respectfully on our understanding of the process, we should remain essentially unified on the ultimate outcome: the glory of God in the salvation, sanctification, transformation, and glorification of His saints.

What Can We Affirm?

The practical application of eschatological opinions varies greatly. It often determines how we view the church, the nation of Israel, the kingdom of God, missions, cultural engagement, ethics, and the political process. One's eschatology may also cause him or her to overemphasize some matters and neglect others.

At minimum, each view should include the following:

Anticipation

Biblical commands to watch, wait, and look up (see Matthew 24:42; 25:12; Luke 12:36-37; 21:28; 1 Thessalonians 5:6; Revelation 16:15) all indicate that we should live in anticipation of the Lord's coming for His own. We are to watch because we don't know the time of His coming (Matthew 24:42; 25:13). He will come "like a thief in the night" (1 Thessalonians 5:2), and He will reward those "who have loved His appearing" (2 Timothy 4:8).

Preparation

In the meantime, believers are to live in preparation for His coming. We are called to be "without stain or reproach until the appearing of our Lord Jesus Christ" (1 Timothy 6:14). Even if we are tested by fire, we may "be found to result in praise and glory and honor at the revelation of Jesus Christ" (1 Peter 1:7). In light of His promised appearing, "everyone who has this hope fixed on Him purifies himself, just as He is pure" (1 John 3:3).

Participation

Jesus told the disciples that they would do "greater works" than He had done because He was going back to heaven to the Father (John 14:12). In the meantime, He instructed them to remain faithful and keep busy serving Him here on earth until He returns (Matthew 24:45-46). In the parable of the talents, Jesus commended the servants who were the most productive while the master was away (Matthew 25:14-30).

Glorification

The ultimate goal of eschatology is the glory of Christ, which will be displayed "when He comes to be glorified in His saints" (2 Thessalonians 1:10). In the meantime, our present sufferings are "not worthy to be compared with the glory that is to be revealed to us" (Romans 8:18) because "when Christ, who is our life, is revealed, then you will also be revealed with Him in glory" (Colossians 3:4). Therefore, God calls us through the gospel that we may "gain the glory of our Lord Jesus Christ" (2 Thessalonians 2:14) because those whom God has called and justified "He also glorified" (Romans 8:30). God's goal for believers is that "He might present to Himself the church in all her glory...that she would be holy and blameless" (Ephesians 5:27).

Any eschatology lacking these elements falls woefully short of a solid biblical understanding of God's future plans and purposes. Beyond these basic elements of eschatology are specific matters of prophetic interpretation that define the details. While we may each differ greatly in these matters, particularly with regard to their practical application, we should treat one another with respect for our common commitment to the ultimate triumph of God's sovereign purposes. There is no place for pejorative comments, oversimplifications, or outright misrepresentations of one another's views.[6]

How Does It Work?

The practical application of eschatology is a result of its basic affirmations. Beyond matters upon which we can all agree are specific interpretive issues related to our beliefs about Israel, the church, the kingdom, the timing of the rapture, the nature of the second coming, the millennial reign of Christ, and the eternal state. In this regard, Michael Bird suggests that the "study of eschatology, with its emphasis on the final kingdom of God, needs to be pushed up much earlier in the theological curriculum."[7] In other words, specific details (such as the rapture, the antichrist, the millennium) need to be viewed in the wider context of biblical and systematic theology.

The ultimate questions have to do with the larger story of the

Bible itself. Alan Bandy (premillennialist) and Benjamin Merkle (amillennialist) comment, "If the Bible truly is God's inspired and infallible Word, and not merely the words of humans, it will naturally present a unified message."[8] This is as true of eschatology as it is of soteriology. The unified message of eschatology is that Jesus is coming again.[9]

The *what* question in generally clear. The *how* question is much more a matter of interpretive debate. For most premillennialists, there is a clear distinction between the church and the kingdom. For amillennialists, they are one and the same. For postmillennialists, the church must continue to grow in order for the kingdom to spread on earth. While many view the latter as a more positive picture of the future of the church, others question this in light of the challenges facing the church in the postmodern world. It should be remembered that the postmillennial dream for the twentieth century as the "Christian century" was interrupted by the Great Depression and two world wars.[10] Thus, every view of eschatology must be measured against the external test of reality. In other words, does this view work in the real world?

Charles Ryrie said of dispensational premillennialism that "it magnifies the grace of God, for it recognizes that true progress can come only from God's gracious intervention in human society."[11] In general, virtually all evangelicals believe God alone can guarantee the future by His divine intervention in human history. *How* He will intervene is a matter of varying opinions. It is not our purpose here to evaluate all those options in detail, but rather, to suggest that pretribulational premillennialism is much more optimistic about the future than its critics tend to suggest.

We are very optimistic about the sovereignty of God, His divine purposes, the power of the gospel, the growth of the church, and the expression of the global Christian mission. We are optimistic about all things divinely ordained and empowered. But, we are realistic optimists. We do not pretend to see progress where there is none.

Much of the world today still lies under the influence of the wicked one. There is much that needs to be done to reach the world with the gospel.

On the other hand, we are pessimistic about all things human. For without the grace of God and the power of divine regeneration, there is little hope for the human race. This does not mean that we abandon the world, but that we face the reality that the "prince of the power of the air" is still a force with which to be reckoned (Ephesians 2:2). Even though his eternal destiny has been judged and determined (John 12:31), he still prowls about seeking whom he may devour (1 Peter 5:8).

Where Does It All Lead?

The ultimate application of any eschatology will determine the practical outcome of its trajectory in society. Dispensationalists take serious note of the failure of human society in the past: the preflood and postflood civilizations, the era of the judges and kings of Israel, and the warnings of a future apostasy (2 Thessalonians 2:3). We also have a very high view of the church, the bride of Christ. We believe that Jesus loves her, gave Himself for her, and will come again to take her to the Father's house before He pours out His wrath on the world.

We do not believe the church will escape persecution, trials, and testing. She has always been the object of the wrath of Satan and the wrath of man. But, we do not believe she will be the object of the wrath of Christ (1 Thessalonians 5:9). Nor do we believe she will be "purified" by the tribulation period in some kind of "Protestant purgatory." It seems incredulous to us that Christ would beat up His bride and then take her to the marriage supper. Our view of the bride (those who are "in Christ") is that she holds a unique place in God's eternal plans and will rule with Him in His earthly kingdom.

Just because we believe in a future rapture does not mean we are escapists who will one day leave this world behind. As premillennialists, we believe we will return to this earth with Christ (Revelation 19:7-9, 14). Unlike those who foresee only a spiritual future, we believe we will participate in a literal earthly kingdom during the millennium. John Feinberg has suggested that we correctly hold a biblical worldview and philosophy of history that emphasizes both the *spiritual* and *physical* implications of God's purposes for this world.[12] Michael Vlach adds, "In this sense, dispensationalists are more holistic in their understanding of God's kingdom purposes" than those who limit His kingdom to the spiritual realm alone.[13]

Philip Ryken states, "Everybody has a worldview. Whether we know it or not, we all have a fundamental perspective on the world that shapes the way we live."[14] The same is true of eschatological views. Our perspective shapes the way we live in the present by what we believe will happen in the future. Those who hold to a posttribulational perspective—who believe the church will go through the tribulation—tend to develop a mindset that urges believers to prepare for persecution. Pretribulationalists, on the other hand, believe the rapture will precede the time of divine wrath and usually hope this rapture will happen soon. By contrast, amillennialists usually view the entire church age as a time of tribulation.

While all pretribulationalists believe the rapture will occur before the tribulation period, that does not mean we believe we will escape trouble or persecution in the meantime. In fact, there is no biblical guarantee that there could not be, for example, a limited nuclear strike prior to the rapture—even against America. What would that mean to the pretrib rapture view? First, the church exists worldwide and is not solely dependent upon its survival in America. Second, if there were an extensive global nuclear war, that wouldn't support anyone's eschatological view! In light of the socio-economic-political issues of our time, all Christians of every eschatological viewpoint need to pray and work for peace and remain active in spreading the gospel and engaging the culture.

The various eschatological perspectives also influence how Christians view the significance of Israel's return to the Promised Land. Premillennialists in general (pre-, mid-, and posttribulationists) usually believe the modern nation of Israel exists in fulfillment of biblical prophecies (Isaiah 35:10; Ezekiel 36:24; Amos 9:15). By contrast, most amillennialists and postmillennialists believe the Christian church has replaced national Israel as the new "Israel" of God. As a result, they often tend to criticize, reject, or overlook Israel's significance today. In this regard, eschatological views have international consequences for Christian involvement. For example, pretribulationalists see great significance in the fact the people of Israel are back in their land, for their presence potentially sets the stage for the fulfillment of the prophecies of the last days. But this does not mean we do not hold national Israel to the same standards as we do other nations of the world.

Pretribulationalists are well aware of the serious issues of our time. We do not run ahead of God's timetable with wild-eyed speculations like *eschatomaniacs*. Also, we do not turn a blind eye to the obvious like *eschatophobics*. Rather, we face the reality that (1) Israel is back in the Promised Land; (2) the Middle East is in social-political-religious turmoil; (3) weapons of mass destruction have already been invented; and (4) the global economy already exists. Thus it certainly seems like the final stage of the eschatological drama has been set. However, the timing is in the Father's hands. Thus, in the meantime, we wait, watch, remain ready, and keep on serving faithfully.

Why Does It Matter?

If eschatology (beliefs about the prophetic future) influences Christian attitudes, practices, and policies, then it matters a great deal. Barry Horner has observed that many nonpremillennialists have expressed a derogatory anti-Judaism in their theological convictions. He notes that some have "inferred that they would be delighted if the Arabs would push Israel into the Mediterranean

Sea, repossess Palestine, and thus vindicate their eschatology!"[15] As a result, these nonpremillennialists ignore, belittle, or distort Israel's prophetic significance. In response, Horner writes, "If a Christian's eschatology produces an indifference, detachment, or even antagonism towards things Jewish...there is something wrong with that eschatological expression."[16]

Horner advocates, as do most premillennialists, an "apostolic compassion" for the Jews in contrast to the growing anti-Semitic and anti-Zionist sentiments so often expressed by many theologians. Pretribulationalists appeal to the apostle Paul's insistence that "God has not rejected His people" (Romans 11:1), and thus our heart's desire and prayer for them to be saved ought to be as passionate as was his (Romans 10:1). In concluding his insightful study and historical survey, Horner insists the "most vital matter in the current debate over the future destiny of national Israel" is the issue of "tone" and "attitude" toward the Jewish people—which is generally a result of one's eschatology.[17]

Eschatology matters because the *end* matters. The message of the Bible moves toward a series of grand conclusions. The Old Testament promises that the "seed of the woman" will ultimately triumph over Satan (see Genesis 3:15). It further narrows that seed to the line of Abraham (Genesis 12:1-3; 15:1-6) and Isaac (Genesis 49:10). Later, God's covenant with David promised him a kingdom, dynasty, and throne forever (2 Samuel 7:12-17). All through the Old Testament the prophets predicted the coming of this ruler, and the Old Testament ends with anticipation for His eventual arrival (Malachi 4:2-6).

The New Testament provides the conclusion: Jesus, the descendant of Abraham and David (Matthew 1:1), is the "King of the Jews" (Matthew 2:2). At His first coming, He called upon the people of Israel to repent because "the kingdom of heaven is at hand" (Matthew 4:17). When they failed to do so, the kingdom promise was postponed until the future (Acts 1:6-7). The New Testament reader is left waiting for the King to return to establish His kingdom on the earth at the second coming, as the book of Revelation promises (19:11-16).

The kingdom of God is a fundamental concept in the New Testament. The expression is found 61 times in the synoptic Gospels. Counting parallels to these passages, the expression occurs more than 85 times.[18] Matthew's Gospel uses the terms "kingdom of God" and "kingdom of heaven" interchangeably (19:23-24). While the term "kingdom" can be used in Scripture to speak of God's sovereign rule over the universe, the New Testament makes it clear that the eschatological kingdom will be inaugurated by the coming of Christ when He returns to earth (Matthew 13:41; 25:31-46).

The future kingdom of God is in view when the Lord taught the disciples to pray, "Your kingdom come. Your will be done, on earth as it is in heaven" (Matthew 6:10). At the last supper, Jesus told His disciples, "Truly I say to you, I will never again drink of the fruit of the vine until that day when I drink it new in the kingdom of God" (Mark 14:25). Matthew's parallel account reads, "I will not drink of this fruit of the vine from now on until that day when I drink it new with you in My Father's kingdom" (Matthew 26:29).

Telling a Better Story

Those of us who hold to the view that the rapture will precede the tribulation believe we have a better story to tell. This is especially important in our postmodern world, where narratives form and express theological ideas. In that sense, the Bible is the story of God. As Christians, we believe it is a better story than other religious books offer because it best explains the human predicament and offers the most helpful solution. Swiss theologian Karl Barth suggested that theology is the "self-examination of the Christian church in respect to its distinctive talk about God."[19] Michael Bird goes a step further, proclaiming that evangelical theology in particular is "the drama of *gospelizing*," by which he means to make and enable Christian disciples to "perform the script of the Scriptures."[20]

This leaves us with a series of important questions regarding our views of eschatology:

1. Does my view give me a love for Christ's appearing?

2. Does it motivate me to action with regard to fulfilling the Great Commission?

3. Does my view help me sort out the details of prophetic events?

4. Does it provide a realistic understanding of the past, present, and future?

5. Am I motivated to be used of God to make a difference in the world today?

6. Does my view give me confidence and hope regarding the future?

7. Am I living in anticipation of Christ's coming for His bride?

For pretribulationalists, it is more important than ever that we understand that when it comes to eschatology we have a better story to tell and a better song to sing.

First, our view of eschatology does a better job of *organizing the biblical data*. We are sincerely trying to put together the pieces of the prophetic puzzle that other views often avoid. Too many approaches to eschatology leave out the difficult details and belittle those who attempt to formulate a clear picture of the future.

Second, we have a message of confident *hope for the future*. We have a high view of the destiny of the church as the bride of Christ. We are convinced the Savior loves her and intends to take her in the rapture before He declares war on the unbelieving world. After He takes us to heaven to the Father's house, we will return with Him in triumph as He puts the bride on display when He returns to earth (Revelation 19:14). Ours is not a message of doom and gloom, but one of "blessed hope" for true believers (Titus 2:13). It is bad news only for the lost, and good news for the saved—which ultimately is the case in all eschatological views.[21]

Third, we have a high view of *Christ's love for the church*. Richard Mayhue writes, "Remember, Christ is coming to a hostile people who will eventually fight against Him at Armageddon. So, the pretribulation rapture best pictures the King rescuing, by a rapture, His faithful followers who are trapped in a hostile world and who will later accompany Him when He returns to conquer His enemies and set up His kingdom."[22]

Fourth, we have a great confidence in *God's eternal purposes*. We are convinced that time is marching on toward a date with divine destiny. God is not helplessly watching the world unravel before Him. He has clearly promised to intervene in the end. Understanding when and how He will do this is viewed differently by various people. We who are pretribulationalists and premillennialists believe we have a *realistic* view of the future. We believe that we have a calling to preach the gospel, win the lost, make disciples, grow the church, and impact the world by the power of God through His Spirit and for His glory until the trumpet sounds.

CHAPTER 12

Are You Ready?

The hope God offers is the only realistic, absolute,
hope that carries the promise of a certain outcome.[1]

DAVID JEREMIAH

The timing of the last days is up to God. But from a human standpoint, it would appear that we are standing on the threshold of the final frontier. We don't think the pieces of the puzzle could be in place any better than they are right now. The stage is now set for the fulfillment of the end-time prophecies, but the timing is in God's hands.

Each of us must plan our lives as though we will live for many more years to come. We have a responsibility to our families, children, grandchildren, and other people around us. But we must also live as though Jesus could return at any moment. It is difficult for non-Christians to understand the balanced approach we must have toward the future. We Christians do not fear the future because we believe God controls it. But at the same time, we do not view it with unbridled optimism.

The tension between living for today and looking forward to tomorrow is one of the realities of the Christian life. Believers find themselves caught in the tension between the here and now and the hereafter. Though we are enjoying our daily walk of faith here on earth, we also have a desire to depart and be with Christ. The apostle Paul spoke about this tension when he wrote, "For to me, to live is Christ and to die is gain" (Philippians 1:21).

Bible prophecy emphasizes that we need to be ready because Christ could come at any moment. Because of the imminence of His return, we must be waiting and watching every moment. At the same time, we have serious responsibilities to fulfill in this world. We cannot use our belief in Christ's return as an excuse to avoid our obligations.

The Bible not only tells us how to prepare for the future, it also tells us how to live right now. It tells us about the destiny of the world's nations, and it also speaks about our personal destiny. As the sand of time slips through the hourglass of eternity, we are all moving closer to an appointment with God.

Once you settle the question of your eternal destiny, you can better determine the present course of your life. Your choices and values will be determined by what is to come. No longer will your decisions be made in light of their immediate consequences; rather, they will be made in light of their eternal significance.

Rather than possessing an escapist mentality, prophecy students have an earnest desire to be ready at all times to meet the Lord, who could come at any moment to call us home. We want to be watching, ready, and serving. That's what our Lord commanded of us in the Olivet Discourse (see Matthew 24:42-46).

A readiness to meet the Lord when He returns is one of the great motivations of the Christian life. First, we must be certain that we know Christ as our Savior. Second, we must live out our faith by being ready to meet Him at any moment. He could come, or we could go, at any time.

What Can We Expect?

Speculating about the future beyond what the Bible itself predicts is a dangerous game. Psychics make countless predictions every year that never come true. But a gullible general public doesn't seem to care. People quickly run out and buy the list of predictions for next year.

Bible prophecy, however, does not work that way. The prophets sent by God made many predictions about the first and second comings of Christ many centuries ago. Their prophecies have stood the test of time, and every single prophecy about the first coming was fulfilled accurately. There are many more prophecies yet to be fulfilled, and we can have full confidence they will come to pass as well:

- The *spread of the gospel and the growth of the church* through the worldwide evangelism of all nations (Matthew 24:14).

- The rise of *religious apostasy* in the last days, leading to widespread sin and lawlessness (2 Thessalonians 2:3).

- The *rapture of the church* (true believers) to heaven prior to the outpouring of God's judgments during the tribulation (Revelation 3:10).

- The *rise of the antichrist and the false prophet* to control the New World Order of the end times (Revelation 13:1-4, 11-18).

- The *triumphal return of Christ* with His church to overthrow the antichrist and bind Satan for 1,000 years (Revelation 19:11-16; 20:1-2).

- The *millennial kingdom* of Christ on earth for 1,000 years of peace and prosperity (Revelation 5:10; 20:4-6).

Beyond these key events, we can only speculate about what will happen. The Bible predicts an age of unparalleled selfism in the last days (2 Timothy 3:1-6). It warns of an age of skepticism and unbelief; a time when people will scoff at the idea of Christ's return (2 Peter 3:3-4). This age will also be marked by global wealth and prosperity (Revelation 18:11-19).

The Bible warns us that humanity is marching toward inevitable destruction. The end might not come now or even in our lifetimes, but it *will* come. Scripture tells us that the great crisis will begin somewhere in the Middle East and eventually spread to the whole world.

The prophet Isaiah warned of a day when God would judge the whole earth (Isaiah 24). He foresaw a time when God would "lay waste the earth and devastate it...The earth will be completely laid waste and totally plundered...The earth dries up and withers, the world languishes...earth's inhabitants are burned up, and very few are left" (Isaiah 24:1-6 NIV).

There can be little doubt that Isaiah is talking about the Great Tribulation, which will culminate in the Battle of Armageddon.[2] He sees a world in which God's wrath is being poured on "all nations" (Isaiah 34:2) and "mountains shall be melted" (Isaiah 34:3 KJV) and the "stars in the sky will be dissolved and the heavens rolled up like a scroll" (Isaiah 34:4).

In both Isaiah 24 and 34, the prophet sees ahead to the time of God's judgment on the whole world. While Scripture records specific judgments on Israel during the "time of Jacob's trouble" and on the kingdom of the antichrist, it also tells us that an even greater judgment will come upon the world at large. No person or place will escape God's retribution at the end time. The apocalyptic holocaust will be worldwide, and no one will be able to hide from what God has waiting for them.

How Will It All End?

The question of *how* all this will come about divides Christians who have differing eschatological views. *Pretribulationalists* believe Christ will rapture the church to heaven prior to the tribulation and then return with His bride at the end of the tribulation to set up His kingdom on earth. *Mid-* and *posttribulationalists* believe the church will suffer to some extent during the tribulation or at the very end of the Great Tribulation.

Amillennialists believe things will get worse at the end of the church age. While most people view the entire church age as a time of tribulation for believers, some feel that the persecution of Christians will get worse in the last days. Amillennialists say that at the very end, the Battle of Armageddon will commence, and Christ will return to judge the world and usher in eternity.

Postmillennialists believe that the church is the kingdom of God on earth and that it is our responsibility to bring in the kingdom by the preaching of the gospel and the enactment of Christian laws, values, and principles in society until the whole world is converted to Christ.

Obviously there are great differences in each of those views, and yet each one contains an element of truth that all Christians need to remember. From the *pretribulationalist* we are reminded to be ready for the coming of Christ at any moment. From the *mid-* and *posttribulationalist* we are reminded that frequently Christians are called to suffer for Christ. Certainly, believers in the Third World could teach us much about what it means to suffer for Christ.

The *amillennialist* reminds us that we must be ready to face the judgment of God. While it is exciting to think about our Lord's coming, we must also realize that His judgment is coming as well. While we premillennialists look forward to Christ's earthly kingdom, we must also remember that even that will come to an end and be merged into the eternal kingdom of God. The apostle Paul says there is coming a time when Christ "hands over the kingdom to God the Father" (1 Corinthians 15:24).

From the *premillennialist* we are reminded of our Christian responsibilities to the world in which we live. Because we do not know the exact time of Christ's return, we dare not sit back and do nothing but wait for the rapture. Christ has given us specific orders about our responsibilities to one another and to the world at large. We are called to be the salt of the earth and the light of the world until our Lord returns (Matthew 5:13-16).

What Should We Be Doing?

Because we can never be sure when God's purpose for His church will be completed, we must remain obedient to our Lord's commands regarding the church. This was made clear to the disciples at the time of Christ's ascension to heaven. They asked Him if He was going to restore the kingdom to Israel at that time, and Jesus told them, "It is not for you to know the times or dates the Father has set by His own authority" (Acts 1:7). Two facts are clear in this statement: (1) The date has been set; and (2) we aren't supposed to know it because we have a responsibility to fulfill in the meantime.

In the very next verse, Jesus gave the Great Commission. He told the disciples they would be empowered by the Holy Spirit to be His witnesses in Jerusalem, Judea, Samaria, and "to the ends of the earth" (verse 8). Then, to their amazement, He ascended into heaven, leaving them gazing intently into the sky. Two men in white (probably angels) appeared and asked, "Why do you stand here looking into the sky? This same Jesus, who has been taken from you into heaven, will come back in the same way you have seen Him go into heaven" (verse 11).

All too often, today's Christians are like the early disciples. We spend more time gazing into the sky and speculating about Christ's return than we do serving Him. The angels' point was to remind the disciples that His return is certain. Thus we shouldn't waste time and energy worrying about when or whether Christ will return. Believe that He is coming again on schedule, and be about His business in the meantime.

Jesus left instructions about what we are to do while we await His coming:

1. *Witness for Him everywhere you go.* Our Lord told His disciples to be His witnesses everywhere they go, even to the farthest ends of the earth (Acts 1:8).

2. *"Go into all the world and preach the gospel"* (Mark 16:15).

This command emphasizes the missionary nature of the church's ministry during the present era. We are to take the gospel to the whole world.

3. *"Repentance for forgiveness of sins would be proclaimed...to all nations"* our Lord declared in Luke 24:47. Calling men and women to repent and believe the gospel is the twofold nature of the evangelistic enterprise.

4. *"Make disciples of all the nations, baptizing them,"* Jesus said in Matthew 28:19. Making converts and discipling them in their walk with God is a major emphasis of the church's mission.

5. *Build the church, not fearing the gates of hell.* Jesus told His disciples that He would build His church with such power that the "gates of hell shall not prevail against it" (Matthew 16:18 KJV). We usually act as though hell were attacking the church and we were trying to survive. But remember, you don't attack with gates. Rather, you defend with them. Jesus portrayed the church as being on the offensive and hell on the defensive.

6. *"Occupy till I come"* (Luke 19:13 KJV), Jesus said in the parable of the talents. In this parable, the servants were to put their master's money to work until the master returned. Likewise, we are to stay busy about the Master's business until He returns.

7. *Remain faithful until He returns.* Our Lord concluded His prophetic message in the Olivet Discourse by urging the disciples to continue in faithful and wise service even though He might be gone for a long time (Matthew 24:45-51; 25:14-21).

How Can We Be Ready?

The hope of the second coming is the strongest encouragement for us to live right until Jesus comes. The apostle John said, "Abide in Him, so that when He appears, we may have confidence and not shrink away from Him in shame at His coming...We know that when He appears, we will be like Him, because we will see Him just as He is. And everyone who has this hope fixed on Him purifies himself, just as He is pure" (1 John 2:28; 3:2-3).

The ultimate incentive to right living is the fact that we will face our Lord when He comes again. No matter what our failures and mistakes in the past, each of us needs to be ready when He comes. How, then, should we live?

First, *you need to know Jesus Christ personally.* The whole purpose of our Lord's first coming was to die as the atoning sacrifice for our sins. He came to pay the price for our sins so that we might be forgiven and released from the penalty of eternal death. He is called the Redeemer because He has freed us from God's judgment against our sin. Peter said, "You were ...redeemed...with precious blood... the blood of Christ...He was foreknown before the foundation of the world, but has appeared in these last times for the sake of you who through Him are believers in God, who raised Him from the dead and gave Him glory, so that your faith and hope are in God" (1 Peter 1:18-21).

Second, *you need to receive Him as your Savior by faith.* We cannot earn salvation by our own good works, nor is it something we deserve. It must be received as a free gift from God. The Bible says, "Christ...died for sins once for all, the just for the unjust, so that He might bring us to God" (1 Peter 3:18). The gospel—the good news—is the message that Christ died for our sins, was buried, and rose again (1 Corinthians 15:3-4). The invitation of the gospel calls us to personal faith in those facts. The Bible says. "As many as received Him, to them He gave the right to become children of God" (John 1:12).

There are many things that demand our attention in life. There are many voices calling to us and many images that flash across the screens of our minds. But no matter what our focus in life, one thing is certain: All of us will face death at some point. We cannot avoid it. We are all vulnerable.

Death is the great equalizer. It makes no difference how rich or poor, famous or infamous, respected or rejected you may have been in this life. When you face death, you are facing an impartial judge. The Bible reminds us that "all have sinned" (Romans 3:23), and that "the wages of sin is death" (Romans 6:23). When death comes knocking at your door, all that really matters is that you are ready to face it.

Perhaps you've heard people talk about Armageddon, the coming of Christ, and the end of the age, and you've realized that you are not ready to meet Christ when He comes. Perhaps you have come to realize that the end could come at any moment, and that you are not prepared to step into eternity.

There is no better time to settle the question of your eternal destiny than right now. John the Baptist called Jesus "the Lamb of God who takes away the sin of the world!" (John 1:29). Won't you let Him take away your sin? Bow your heart, soul, and mind before Him, and ask Him to save you right now.

When Billy Graham was asked on a popular television show to summarize what his life and ministry were all about, he quoted John 3:16: "God so loved the world, that He gave His only begotten Son, that whoever believes in Him shall not perish, but have eternal life."

Bible prophecy was not written to scare us. It was written to prepare us to come to Christ while there is still time. The clock of human history is ticking away. It neither speeds up nor slows down. It just keeps on ticking continually and relentlessly, moving us closer and closer to the end of the age. How close we are to the end will be revealed only by time itself. Don't gamble with your eternal destiny. Your time may very well be running out. Make sure you are ready when Jesus comes, for "in a very little while, He who is coming will come, and will not delay" (Hebrews 10:37).

50 Reasons for Pretribulationism
Dr. John F. Walvoord

B elow is an adapted summary of 50 arguments for pretribulationism, which originally appeared in Dr. John Walvoord's book *The Rapture Question.*

Historical Reasons

1. The early church believed in the imminency of the Lord's return, which is an essential doctrine of pretribulationism.

2. The detailed development of pretribulational truth during the past few centuries does not prove that the doctrine is new or novel. Its development is similar to that of other major doctrines in the history of the church.

Hermeneutics

3. Pretribulationism is the only view which allows a literal interpretation of all Old and New Testament passages on the great tribulation.

4. Only pretribulationism distinguishes clearly between Israel and the church and their respective programs.

The Nature of the Tribulation

5. Pretribulationism maintains the scriptural distinction between the great tribulation and tribulation in general which precedes it.

6. The great tribulation is properly interpreted by pretribulationists as a time of preparation for Israel's restoration (Deut. 4:29-30; Jer. 30:4-11). It is not the purpose of the tribulation to prepare the church for glory.

7. None of the Old Testament passages on the tribulation mention the church (Deut. 4:29-30; Jer. 30:4-11; Dan. 9:24-27; 12:1-2).

8. None of the New Testament passages on the tribulation mention the church (Matt. 24:15-31; 1 Thess. 1:9-10; 5:4-9; Rev. 4-19).

9. In contrast to midtribulationism, the pretribulational view provides an adequate explanation for the beginning of the great tribulation in Revelation 6. Midtribulationism is refuted by the plain teaching of Scripture that the great tribulation begins long before the seventh trumpet of Revelation 11.

10. The proper distinction is maintained between the prophetic trumpets of Scripture by pretribulationism. There is no proper ground for the pivotal argument of midtribulationism that the seventh trumpet of Revelation is the last trumpet in that there is no established connection between the seventh trumpet of

Revelation 11, the last trumpet of 1 Corinthians 15:52, and the trumpet of Matthew 24:31. They are three distinct events.

11. The unity of Daniel's seventieth week is maintained by pretribulationists. By contrast, midtribulationism destroys the unity of Daniel's seventieth week and confuses Israel's program with that of the church.

The Nature of the Church

12. The translation of the church is never mentioned in any passage dealing with the second coming of Christ after the tribulation.

13. The church is not appointed to wrath (Rom. 5:9; 1 Thess. 1:9-10; 5:9). The church therefore cannot enter "the great day of their wrath" (Rev. 6:17).

14. The church will not be overtaken by the Day of the Lord (1 Thess. 5:1-9), which includes the tribulation.

15. The possibility of a believer escaping the tribulation is mentioned in Luke 21:36.

16. The church of Philadelphia was promised deliverance from the "hour of trial, that hour which is to come upon the whole world, to try them that dwell upon the earth" (Rev. 3:10).

17. It is characteristic of divine dealing to deliver believers before a divine judgment is inflicted upon the world as illustrated in the deliverance of Noah, Lot, Rahab, etc. (2 Pet. 2:6-9).

18. At the time of the translation of the church, all believers go to the Father's house in heaven, and do not remain on the earth as taught by posttribulationists (John 14:3).

19. Pretribulationism does not divide the body of Christ at the rapture on a works principle. The teaching of a partial rapture is based on the false doctrine that the translation of the church is a reward for good works. It is rather a climactic aspect of salvation by grace.

20. The Scriptures clearly teach that all, not part, of the church will be raptured at the coming of Christ for the church (1 Cor. 15:51-52; 1 Thess. 4:17).

21. As opposed to a view of a partial rapture, pretribulationism is founded on the definite teaching of Scripture that the death of Christ frees from all condemnation.

22. The godly remnant of the tribulation are pictured as Israelites, not members of the church as maintained by the posttribulationists.

23. The pretribulational view as opposed to posttribulationism does not confuse general terms like *elect* and *saints*, which apply to the saved of all ages with specific terms like *the church* and those *in Christ*, which refer to believers of this age only.

The Doctrine of Imminency

24. The pretribulational interpretation is the only view which teaches that the coming of Christ is actually imminent.

25. The exhortation to be comforted by the coming of the Lord (1 Thess. 4:18) is significant only in the pretribulational view, and is especially contradicted by posttribulationism.

26. The exhortation to look for "the glorious appearing"

(Titus 2:13) loses its significance if the tribulation must intervene first. Believers, in that case, should look for signs.

27. The exhortation to purify ourselves in view of the Lord's return has most significance if His coming is imminent (1 John 3:2-3).

28. The church is uniformly exhorted to look for the coming of the Lord, while believers in the tribulation are directed to look for signs.

The Work of the Holy Spirit

29. The Holy Spirit as the restrainer of evil cannot be taken out of the world unless the church, which the Spirit indwells, is translated at the same time. The tribulation cannot begin until this restraint is lifted.

30. The Holy Spirit as the restrainer must be taken out of the world before "the lawless one," who dominates the tribulation period, can be revealed (2 Thess. 2:6-8).

31. If the expression "except the falling away come first" be translated literally "except the departure come first," it would plainly show the necessity of the rapture taking place before the beginning of the tribulation.

The Necessity of an Interval Between the Rapture and Second Coming

32. According to 2 Corinthians 5:10, all believers of this age must appear before the judgment seat of Christ in heaven, an event never mentioned in the detailed accounts connected with the second coming of Christ to earth.

33. If the 24 elders of Revelation 4:1–5:14 are representative of the church, as many expositors believe, it would necessitate the rapture and reward of the church before the tribulation.

34. The marriage of Christ and the church must be celebrated in heaven before the second coming to the earth (Rev. 19:7-10).

35. Tribulation saints are not translated at the second coming of Christ, but will carry on ordinary occupations such as farming and building houses, and they will also bear children (Isa. 65:20-25). This would be impossible if all saints were translated at the second coming to the earth, as posttribulationists teach.

36. The judgment of the Gentiles following the second coming (Matt. 25:31-46) indicates that both saved and unsaved are still in their natural bodies, which would be impossible if the translation had taken place at the second coming.

37. If the translation took place in connection with the second coming to the earth, there would be no need to separate the sheep from the goats at a subsequent judgment, but the separation would have taken place in the very act of the translation of the believers before Christ actually came to the earth.

38. The judgment of Israel (Ezek. 20:34-38), which occurs subsequent to the second coming, indicates the necessity of regathering Israel. The separation of the saved from the unsaved in this judgment obviously takes place sometime after the second coming and would be unnecessary if a translation of the saved had taken place previously.

Contrasts Between the Rapture and the Second Coming

39. At the time of the rapture the saints meet Christ in the air, while at the second coming Christ returns to the Mount of Olives to meet the saints on earth.

40. At the time of the rapture the Mount of Olives is unchanged, while at the second coming it divides and a valley is formed to the east of Jerusalem (Zech. 14:4-5).

41. At the rapture living saints are translated, while no saints are translated in connection with the second coming of Christ to the earth.

42. At the rapture the saints go to heaven, while at the second coming to the earth the saints remain on the earth without translation.

43. At the time of the rapture the world is unjudged and continues in sin, while at the second coming the world is judged and righteousness is established on the earth.

44. The translation of the church is pictured as a deliverance before the day of wrath, while the second coming is followed by the deliverance of those who have believed in Christ during the tribulation.

45. The rapture is described as imminent, while the second coming is preceded by definite signs.

46. The translation of living believers is a truth revealed only in the New Testament, while the second coming with its attendant events is a prominent doctrine of both Testaments.

47. The rapture concerns only the saved, while the second coming deals with both saved and unsaved.

48. At the rapture Satan is not bound, while at the second coming Satan is bound and cast into the abyss.

49. No unfulfilled prophecy stands between the church and the rapture, while many signs must be fulfilled before the second coming.

50. No passage dealing with the resurrection of saints at the second coming ever mentions a translation of living saints at the same time.

Bibliography

Allen, David, and Steve Lemke, eds. *The Return of Christ: A Premillennial Perspective*. Nashville: B&H, 2011.

Bandy, Alan S., and Benjamin L. Merkle. *Understanding Prophecy*. Grand Rapids: Kregel, 2015.

Bingham, J., and G. Kreider. *Eschatology: Biblical, Historical, and Practical Approaches*. Grand Rapids: Kregel, 2016.

Blomberg, Craig, and Sung Wook Chung, eds. *A Case for Historic Premillennialism*. Grand Rapids: Baker, 2009.

Bock, Darrell, ed. *Three Views on the Millennium and Beyond*. Grand Rapids: Zondervan, 1999.

Currie, David. *Rapture: The End-Times Error That Leaves the Bible Behind*. Manchester, NH: Sophia Institute Press, 2003.

DeMar, Gary. *End Times Fiction*. Nashville: Thomas Nelson, 2001.

Frazier, T.L. *A Second Look at the Second Coming*. Ben Lomond, CA: Conciliar Press, 1999.

Gundry, Stanley, ed. *Three Views on the Rapture*. Grand Rapids: Zondervan, 2010.

Hallowell, Billy. *The Armageddon Code*. Lake Mary, FL: Frontline, 2016.

Hanegraaff, Hank. *The Apocalypse Code*. Nashville: Thomas Nelson, 2007.

Hart, John. *Answers to the Most Important Questions About the End Times*. Minneapolis: Bethany House, 2016.

———, ed. *Evidence for the Rapture*. Chicago: Moody, 2015.

Hays, Daniel, Scott Duvall, and Marvin Pate. *Dictionary of Biblical Prophecy and End Times*. Grand Rapids: Zondervan, 2007.

Hindson, Ed. *Earth's Final Hour*. Eugene, OR: Harvest House, 1999.

———. *Final Signs*. Eugene, OR: Harvest House, 1996.

———. *Revelation: Unlocking the Future*. Chattanooga, TN: AMG, 2002.

Hitchcock, Mark. *The Complete Book of Bible Prophecy*. Wheaton, IL: Tyndale House, 1999.

———. *The End*. Carol Stream, IL: Tyndale House, 2012.

Hitchcock, Mark, and Thomas Ice. *Breaking the Apocalypse Code*. Costa Mesa, CA: The Word for Today, 2007.

———. *The Truth Behind Left Behind*. Sisters, OR: Multnomah, 2004.

Hocking, David. *The Case for Pre-Tribulationalism*. Tustin, CA: HFT Publications, 2005.

Ice, Thomas, and Timothy Demy. *The Return*. Grand Rapids: Kregel, 1999.

———. *When The Trumpet Sounds*. Eugene, OR: Harvest House, 1995.

Jeremiah, David. *Is This the End?*. Nashville: Thomas Nelson, 2016.

LaHaye, Tim. *Rapture Under Attack*. Sisters, OR: Multnomah, 1998.

LaHaye, Tim, and Ed Hindson, eds. *The Popular Encyclopedia of Bible Prophecy*. Eugene, OR: Harvest House, 2004.

LaHaye, Tim, Thomas Ice, and Ed Hindson, eds. *The Popular Handbook on the Rapture*. Eugene, OR: Harvest House, 2011.

MacArthur, John, and Richard Mayhue. *Christ's Prophetic Plans.* Chicago: Moody, 2012.

MacPherson, Dave. *The Great Rapture Hoax.* Fletcher, NC: New Puritan Library, 1983.

McKeever, J. *Christians Will Go Through the Tribulation.* Medford, OR: Omega, 1978.

Middleton, J.R. *A New Heaven and a New Earth.* Grand Rapids: Baker, 2014.

Pate, Marvin. *Interpreting Revelation.* Grand Rapids: Kregel, 2016.

Rosenthal, Marvin. *The Pre-Wrath Rapture of the Church.* Nashville: Thomas Nelson, 1990.

Schnabel, Eckhard. *40 Questions About the End Times.* Grand Rapids: Kregel, 2011.

Showers, Renald. *The Pre-Wrath Rapture View.* Grand Rapids: Kregel, 2001.

Sproul, R.C. *The Last Days According to Jesus.* Grand Rapids: Baker, 1998.

Walls, Jerry, ed. *The Oxford Handbook of Eschatology.* Oxford: Oxford University Press, 2008.

Walvoord, John. *The Rapture Question.* Grand Rapids: Zondervan, 1979.

Glossary

Amillennialism   The view of eschatology that teaches there is *no* future rapture or literal 1,000-year reign of Christ on earth. Most believe the spiritual form of the kingdom is present now.

Antichrist   The anti-Christian ruler who comes to power in the last days. Also called the beast in the book of Revelation. The term may be applied to both an individual and the system he represents.

Apostasy   From the Greek *apostasia*, translated "apostasy" (NASB), "rebellion" (NIV), or "falling away" (KJV). Also described as "some shall depart from the faith" (1 Timothy 4:1 KJV).

Armageddon   The term used only in Revelation 16:16 for the final conflict between Christ (the Lamb) and antichrist (the beast). Occurs at the second coming of Christ (Revelation 19:11-16).

Blessed hope   The joyous anticipation (Greek, *makaria elpida*) of the coming of Christ to rapture believers to heaven (Titus 2:13).

Church age   The church (Greek, *ekklesia*) began on the Day of Pentecost (Acts 2) and will culminate at the rapture (1 Thessalonians 4:13-17). During this time Jesus promised to continue to build the church (Matthew 16:16).

Covenants   Agreements mediated between God and humans for specific purposes. Noah, Abraham, Moses, and David specifically received covenant promises in addition to the new covenant predicted by Jeremiah (31:31-34) and instituted by Christ.

Day of the Lord   The biblical term for God's vindication of His righteousness. It is clearly a day of judgment (Joel 2:11; Zephaniah 1:14; Malachi 4:5). It can describe both an imminent future event or the ultimate eschatological consummation.

Dispensationalism   A system of biblical interpretation that distinguishes God's progressive interventions in human history through specific acts of creation and redemption. The term *dispensation* translates the Greek *oikonomia*, often rendered "administration" or "stewardship."

Eschatology   The area of systematic theology concerning the study of future events or last things. It generally encompasses the topics related to the second coming of Christ, the rapture, the resurrection of the dead, the millennial kingdom, the final judgment, and the eternal state.

False prophet   Religious leader of a global spiritual deception designed to promote the worldwide worship of the antichrist in the end times.

Glorious appearing   Christ's coming in glory to the earth with His saints and angels. This will initiate the final phase of His ultimate victory over Satan, the antichrist, and the false prophet (Revelation 19:11-20).

Harpazō   The Greek term for "caught up" or "snatched." The biblical term for the rapture of the church saints (believers).

Imminence   The concept that Christ could come at any time. In relation to the rapture, it means that no biblically predicted prophetic event must necessarily precede it.

Israel   The land of the Jewish people, both ancient and modern. The name ascribed to the descendants of Jacob and the sociopolitical entity of their twelve tribes. Used over 2,000 times in the OT and 74 times in the NT.

Jerusalem   The capital of the state of Israel. Mentioned over 800 times in the Bible (660 in the OT and 142 in the NT). Also called Zion, Salem, Ariel, and the City of David.

Kingdom of God   Both eternal and temporal. The eternal kingdom is timeless, universal, and miraculous. It exists from eternity past until eternity future (1 Corinthians 15:23-28) and represents God's sovereign rule over the entire universe. Its temporal aspects represent God's theocratic rule both in Old Testament Israel and the future millennial reign.

Last days   Biblically this term can refer to either the current church age (Hebrews 1:1-2) or the future culmination of God's plan for Israel (Daniel 12:4). It is generally used in popular terminology to refer to the final days before the rapture or the coming of Christ.

Midtribulationalism   The view that believes Jesus will return in the *middle* of the seven-year tribulation period to rapture the church (believers).

Millennium   The English form of the Latin terms *mille* ("one thousand") and *anum* ("year"). Translates the Greek *chilias*, also meaning "one thousand." Used six times in Revelation 20 (verses 2, 3, 4, 5, 6, 7) to describe the future reign of Christ on earth after His return.

New Jerusalem   The abode of God and the heavenly home of all believers. Referred to as "the heavenly Jerusalem" (Hebrews 12:22); the "holy city" that comes "down out of heaven from God" (Revelation 21:2, 10).

Olivet Discourse   Jesus's longest prophetic sermon, recorded in Matthew 24–25, Mark 13, and Luke 21. It includes both His prediction of the destruction of the temple and the prediction of the signs of His coming after the great tribulation (Matthew 24:29-30).

Partial rapture   The theory that suggests only obedient believers who are deemed worthy will be taken in the rapture.

Postmillennialism   Belief that Christ will return *after* the millennium of the current age, which is not limited to 1,000 years.

Posttribulationalism   Belief that Christ will rapture the church *after* it has gone through the tribulation.

Premillennialism   The belief that Christ will return *before* He establishes a literal millennial reign on earth.

Preterism   The belief that all (or most) prophecies were already fulfilled in the *past* by the time of the destruction of Jerusalem in AD 70.

Pretribulationalism   The view that Christ will return to rapture the church *before* the time of tribulation.

Prewrath   View that teaches the rapture will occur during the tribulation period at the time of the sixth and seventh seal judgments.

Progressive dispensationalism   Differs from traditional dispensationalism by advocating that Christ has already inaugurated the Davidic reign in heaven.

Rapture   From the Greek *harpazō*, meaning "caught up" or "snatched away." Refers to both the resurrection of the "dead in Christ" and those who are still living when Jesus comes in the clouds (1 Thessalonians 4:13-18).

Second coming   The general term for the coming (Greek, *parousia*) of Christ. Includes two phases: the rapture of believers into the air (1 Thessalonians 4:13-18) and Christ's return with them to the earth (Revelation 19:11-21).

Signs of the times   Both the earthly and cosmic signs that will precede the return of Christ to the earth (Luke 21:25-28).

Times of the Gentiles   The period of time from the Babylonian captivity onward during which Israel was subject to the Gentile world powers.

Tribulation   Period of time equated with the final 7 years of the prophecy of the 70 "weeks" or "sevens" (Daniel 9:24-27). A time of divine wrath, trouble, and distress (Matthew 24:9, 21-31) prior to the return of Christ.

Vengeance   From the Greek *ekdikasis*. A technical term for "vindicate" in "judgment." Used 14 times in the NT to refer to God's severe judgments.

Wrath   From the Greek *thumos* ("burning anger") and *orge* ("indignation") poured out by God on the "sons of disobedience" (Ephesians 5:6). Technical terms for the tribulation period as an expression of the wrath of God (Revelation 15:1) and the wrath of Christ the Lamb (Revelation 6:16-17).

Notes

Chapter 1: Rapture Under Attack

1. Barbara R. Rossing, *The Rapture Exposed* (New York: Basic Books, 2004), 1.

2. Rossing, *The Rapture Exposed*.

3. Hank Hanegraaff, *The Apocalypse Code* (Nashville: Thomas Nelson, 2007), xxi.

4. Hanegraaff, *The Apocalypse Code*, xxii.

5. For a thorough discussion see Michael Bird, *Evangelical Theology* (Grand Rapids: Zondervan, 2013), 288-97.

6. David Jeremiah, *Is This the End?* (Nashville: Thomas Nelson, 2016); John MacArthur, *Because the Time Is Near* (Chicago: Moody, 2007); John Hagee, *Final Dawn over Jerusalem* (Nashville: Thomas Nelson, 1998); R.C. Sproul, *The Last Days According to Jesus* (Grand Rapids: Baker, 1998); John Piper, "Bible Prophecy," *Desiring God*, http://www.desiringgod.org/topics/bible-prophecy/all; D.A. Carson and Tim Keller, eds. *The Gospel as Center* (Wheaton, IL: Crossway, 2012).

7. N.T. Wright, "Farewell to the Rapture," *Bible Review*, August 2001. Accessed at http:// ntwrightpage.com/2016/07/12/farewell-to-the-rapture/.

8. Wright, "Farewell to the Rapture."

9. N.T. Wright, *Jesus and the Victory of God* (Philadelphia: Fortress, 1996).

10. From the conclusion of the Nicene Creed.

11. Cf. Max King, *The Cross and the Parousia of Christ* (Warren, OH: Writing and Research Ministry, 1987) and Stuart Russell, *The Parousia* (Grand Rapids: Baker, 1983). Oddly, preterists often suggest either a spiritual or unnoticed ("secret") rapture at AD 70! Cf. R.C. Sproul, *The Last Days According to Jesus* (Grand Rapids: Baker, 1998), 167.

12. Sproul, *The Last Days According to Jesus*, 228.

13. Kenneth Gentry, *The Beast of Revelation* (Tyler, TX: Institute for Christian Economics, 1989).

14. Norman Geisler, "A Review of Hank Hanegraaff's Book, *The Apocalypse Code*," http://normangeisler.com/a-review-of-hanegraaff-apocalypse-code/. Cf. also Mark Hitchcock, "Revelation, Date of," in Tim LaHaye and Ed Hindson, eds. *Popular Encyclopedia of Bible Prophecy* (Eugene, OR: Harvest House, 2004), 336-39.

15. "Life in 2050: Amazing Science, Familiar Trends," *The Pew Research Center*, June 22, 2010, 14-16, http://www.people-press.org/files/legacy-pdf/625.pdf.

16. Cf. Bird, *Evangelical Theology*, 291-300. See also Alan Bundy and Benjamin Merkle, *Understanding Prophecy* (Grand Rapids: Kregel, 2015), 257-60.

17. Stoyan Zaimov, "12 Worst Christian Persecution Nations; US Makes List for First Time," ChristianPost.com, January 4, 2017, http://www.christianpost.com/news/12-worst-christian-persecution-nations-us-makes-list-for-first-time-172551/. The actual report can be found at http://www.persecution.org/persecutionnl/201701/ICC%202016%20Hall%20of%20Shame%20Report.pdf.

18. Mike Bickle, *God's Answer to the Growing Crisis* (Lake Mary, FL: Charisma House, 2016).

19. Gary Burge, "Why I'm not a Christian Zionist, Academically Speaking," http://www.christianzionism.org/article.burge02.pdf (accessed April 15, 2014).

20. Norman Geisler, *Systematic Theology* (Minneapolis: Bethany House, 2005), 4:633.

21. Tim LaHaye, *Who Will Face the Tribulation?* (Eugene, OR: Harvest House, 2003), 19.

22. Norman Geisler, "Why Hold to a Pre-Mill View?" http://normangeisler.com/category/premillenialism/.

Chapter 2: Separating Fact from Fiction

1. Erwin Lutzer, *The King Is Coming* (Chicago: Moody, 2012), 12.

2. Edgar Whisenant, *88 Reasons Why the Rapture Will Be in 1988* (Nashville: World Bible Society, 1988).

3. The Korean *Hyoo-go* movement believed God had revealed the date of Christ's return as being October 1992—this revelation was allegedly given to 12-year-old Bang Ik-Ha. Eugene Taylor, *Psychology Today* (November/December, 1994), 56.

4. J.M. Hile, *Timeline 2000* (Makilteo, WA: WinePress, 1998).

5. Harold Camping, *1994?* (New York: Vantage, 1992).

6. Jose Arguelles, "The Mayan Factor," in *The Mystery of 2012* (Boulder, CO: Sounds True, 2007). Contra, cf. Mark Hitchcock, *2012: The Bible and the End of the World* (Eugene, OR: Harvest House, 2009).

7. John Hagee, *Four Blood Moons* (Franklin, TN: Worthy, 2013). Contra cf. Mark Hitchcock, *Blood Moons Rising: Bible Prophecy, Israel, and the Four Blood Moons* (Carol Stream, IL: Tyndale House, 2014).

8. Cf. W. Lamb, *Signs of the Times* (Sydney, Australia: Advent Herald, 1929), 230-50; H. Rimmer, *Shadow of Coming Events* (Grand Rapids: Eerdmans, 1946); Richard Abanes, *End Time Visions* (Nashville: B&H, 1998).

9. *Zeitgeist* typically means the "spirit of the times." The term was originally coined by Johann Herder in 1769 and is developed by Hegel in his *Phanomenologie des Geists*. It is typically used to describe the general mindset of the culture at a particular time. See N.L. Geisler and P. Feinberg, *Introduction to Philosophy* (Grand Rapids: Baker, 1980), 103-18 and "Hegel, G.W.F." in W.C. Campbell-Jack and G. McGrath, eds. *New Dictionary of Christian Apologetics* (Downers Grove, IL: IVP, 2006), 300-01; R.M. Martin, "Zeitgeist," in *Philosopher's Dictionary*, 3rd ed. (Orchard Park, NY: Broadview Press, 2003), 328.

10. Daniel Mitchell, "Is the Rapture on Schedule?" *National Liberty Journal* (October 1988), 66.

11. Alan Bandy and Benjamin Merkle, *Understanding Prophecy* (Grand Rapids: Kregel, 2015), 33. They emphasize locating prophecy within its original context as an essential step in understanding its meaning. They write, "Once the prophecy is framed, interpreted, and applied in terms of what it *meant*, then we may explore what it *means* for us today."

12. Joel Richardson, *The Islamic Antichrist* (Long Beach, CA: WND Books, 2009). Contra David Reagan, "An Evaluation of the Muslim Antichrist Theory," http://www.pre-trib.org/data/pdf/Reagan-AnEvaluationoftheMusl.pdf.

13. One of the most extreme examples of excessive prophetic speculation is J.R. Church, *Hidden Prophecies in the Psalms* (Oklahoma City, OK: Prophecy

Publications, 1986). He found British general Allenby in Psalm 17 conquering Jerusalem in 1917; Psalm 39–44 telling the story of the Holocaust from 1939–1944; and Psalm 48 predicting the rebirth of Israel in 1948.

14. Cf. Ed Dobson and Ed Hindson, "Armageddon Theology: Preaching, Politics, and the End of the World," in *The Seduction of Power* (Old Tappan, NJ: Revell, 1988), 77-92.

15. See Jonathan Schell, *Fate of the Earth* (Redwood City, CA: Stanford University, 2000).

16. See Andreas Kostenberger, Darrell Bock, and Josh Chatraw, *Truth in a Culture of Doubt* (Nashville: B&H, 2014).

17. Steven McAvoy, "Some Problems with Postribulationism," http://www.pretrib.org/articles/view/some-problems-with-postribulationism.

18. See discussion in Wayne House and Thomas Ice, *Dominion Theology: Blessing or Curse?* (Portland: Multnomah, 1988).

19. This concern has been emphasized in a graphic way in such bestselling novels as Frank Peretti, *This Present Darkness* (Westchester, IL: Crossway, 1986) and Tim LaHaye and Craig Parshall, *Thunder of Heaven* (Grand Rapids: Zondervan, 2011).

20. See discussion in W.H. Swatos, ed., *Encyclopedia of Religion and Society* (Walnut Creek, CA: AltaMira Press, 1998), 562.

21. R. Albert Mohler Jr., "Biblical Theology and the Sexuality Crisis," http://www.albertmohler.com/2014/09/16/biblical-theology-and-the-sexuality-crisis/. A similar concern is raised by David Jeremiah, "The Age of Anything Goes," in *Is This the End?* (Nashville: Thomas Nelson, 2016), 3-30.

22. Duncan Campbell, *Revival in the Hebrides* (Charleston, SC: CreateSpace, 2016), 57.

23. David Jeremiah, *Is This the End?* (Nashville: W Publishing Group, 2016), 125.

24. Richard Abanes, *End-Time Visions* (New York: Four Walls Eight Windows, 1998), 81-111, 209-54. Abanes points out several examples including Adventists (1844), Jehovah's Witnesses (1914), and numerous other evangelical extremists.

25. See Tim LaHaye and Ed Hindson, eds., *Exploring Bible Prophecy from Genesis to Revelation* (Eugene, OR: Harvest House, 2004).

Chapter 3: Raptures in the Bible

1. William Mounce, "Snatch," in W.D. Mounce, *Mounce's Complete Dictionary of Old & New Testament Words* (Grand Rapids: Zondervan, 2006), 666.

2. Anthony A. Hoekema, *The Bible and the Future*, rev. ed. (Grand Rapids: Eerdmans, 1979), 164.

3. Marvin J. Rosenthal, *The Pre-Wrath Rapture of the Church* (Nashville: Thomas Nelson, 1990).

4. Robert H. Gundry, *The Church and the Tribulation* (Grand Rapids: Zondervan, 1990).

5. Robert Govett originated this view in his book *Entrance into the Kingdom: The Apocalypse Expounded by Scripture*, public domain, 1835.

6. Cf. Erich Tiedtke, "Snatch, Take Away, Rapture," in Colin Brown, *New International Dictionary of New Testament Theology* (Grand Rapids: Zondervan, 1971), 3:601-05.

7. A different person named Enoch, a descendant of Cain, is mentioned in Genesis 4:17-18.

8. John Sailhamer, *The Pentateuch as Narrative: A Biblical-Theological Commentary* (Grand Rapids: Zondervan, 1995), 118.

9. See "Enoch," in A.C. Meyers, *Eerdmans Bible Dictionary* (Grand Rapids: Eerdmans, 1987), 336.

10. H.C. Leupold, *Exposition of Genesis* (Columbus, OH: Wartburg Press, 1972), 241.

11. Leupold, *Exposition of Genesis*, 243. Leupold also points out that the rapture ("translation") involved immediate glorification (244).

12. G.Ch. Aalders, *Genesis*, Bible Student's Commentary (Grand Rapids: Zondervan, 1981), 1:141.

13. John Calvin, *A Commentary on Genesis* (London: Banner of Truth, 1965), 1:231.

14. This appears to be a quote from the noncanonical book 1 Enoch 1:9. Douglas Moo, "Jude," in Clinton Arnold, ed. *Zondervan Illustrated Bible Backgrounds Commentary* (Grand Rapids: Zondervan, 2002). 4:241. Moo writes that "most interpreters rightly note that Jude never calls 1 Enoch 'Scripture' (*graphe*). While using the book in his letter, he never accords it canonical

status...But his use of the verb 'prophesy' suggests that he did think that 1 Enoch included at this point a genuine prophecy from Enoch."

15. "Elijah," in *Eerdmans Bible Dictionary*, 325-27.

16. C.F. Keil and Franz Delitzsch, *Biblical Commentary on the Old Testament* (Grand Rapids: Eerdmans 1965), "Books of the Kings," 294.

17. Keil and Delitzsch, "Books of the Kings," 295.

18. John F. Maile, "The Ascension in Luke-Acts." *Tyndale Bulletin* 37 (1986): 29-59.

19. F.F. Bruce, *Commentary on the Book of Acts*, NICNT (Grand Rapids: Eerdmans 1964), 40-41. He suggests the cloud in each case is probably to be interpreted as the shekinah glory.

20. Darrell Bock, *Acts*, BECNT (Grand Rapids: Baker, 2007), 68.

21. J. Dwight Pentecost, *The Words and Works of Jesus Christ* (Grand Rapids: Zondervan, 1981), 513.

22. Bock, *Acts*, 341.

23. Walter Elwell, *Baker Encyclopedia of the Bible* (Grand Rapids: Baker, 1988), 2:1676.

24. Bock, *Acts*, 346.

25. John R.W. Stott, *The Message of Acts* (Downers Grove, IL: IVP, 1990), 162.

26. Stott, *The Message of Acts*.

27. Olaf Moe, *The Apostle Paul: His Message and Doctrine* (Minneapolis: Augsburg, 1954), 1.

28. F.F. Bruce, *Paul: Apostle of the Heart Set Free* (Grand Rapids: Eerdmans, 1977), 16.

29. P.E. Hughes, *Paul's Second Epistle to the Corinthians*, NICNT (Grand Rapids: Eerdmans, 1962), 429.

30. Dan Mitchell, *Second Corinthians: Grace under Siege* (Chattanooga, TN: AMG Publishers, 2008), 188.

31. Mitchell, *Second Corinthians*, 189.

32. John Drane, *Paul* (New York: Harper & Row, 1976), 118.

33. John Walvoord, *The Revelation of Jesus Christ* (Chicago: Moody, 1966), 103.

34. Walvoord, *The Revelation of Jesus Christ.*

35. Robert Thomas, *Revelation 1–7: An Exegetical Commentary* (Chicago: Moody, 1992), 333-37.

36. In Revelation, "overcomers" in the churches are promised white robes (3:5), crowns (3:11), and thrones (3:21).

37. See Ed Hindson, *Revelation: Unlocking the Future* (Chattanooga, TN: AMG Publishers, 2002), 134-37. The "woman" is represented as the mother of Christ, not the bride of Christ, so she cannot symbolize the church. Rather, she is the symbol of Israel and the ancestral line of Christ who descended from Abraham and David (Matthew 1:1).

38. Erich Tiedtke, "Snatch, Take Away, Rapture," 3:603.

Chapter 4: Rapture Views—It's About Time

1. Francis Schaeffer, *Twenty-Five Basic Bible Studies* (Huémoz, Switzerland: L'ABRI Fellowship, nd), 48.

2. Billy Hallowell, "Is the Rapture Really Biblical? Pastors Reveal Exactly Where They Stand on Revelation, Eschatology and 'Left Behind' Theology," *The Blaze*, May 3, 2016, http://www.theblaze.com/stories/2016/05/03/is-the-end-times-rapture-really-in-the-bible-pastors-reveal-exactly-where-they-stand-as-the-eschatology-battle-forges-on/.

3. Renald Showers, *Maranatha Our Lord, Come!* (Bellmawr, NJ: Friends of Israel, 1995), 255.

4. Showers, *Maranatha Our Lord, Come!*, 256.

5. Eckhard Schnabel, *40 Questions About the End Times* (Grand Rapids: Kregel, 2011), 93.

6. Schnabel, *40 Questions About the End Times*, 96, 101.

7. Paul N. Benware, *Understanding End Times Prophecy* (Chicago: Moody, 1995), 216.

8. Gleason L. Archer, "Mid-Seventieth Week Rapture," in *The Rapture: Pre-, Mid-, or Post-Tribulational?* (Grand Rapids: Zondervan, 1984), 139.

9. J. Oliver Buswell Jr., *A Systematic Theology of the Christian Religion*, vol. 2 (Grand Rapids: Zondervan, 1962), 397. Buswell also appeals to the catching

up of the two witnesses in Revelation 11:11-12 as a representation of the rapture due to its close connection to the seventh trumpet. J. Daniel Hays, J. Scott Duvall, and C. Marvin Pate, *Dictionary of Biblical Prophecy and End Times* (Grand Rapids: Zondervan, 2007), 285. Archer, a midtrib advocate, rejects Buswell's identification of the rapture with the two witnesses in Revelation 11. Gleason L. Archer, "Mid-Seventieth Week Rapture," in *The Rapture: Pre-, Mid-, or Post-Tribulational?*, 144.

10. Benware, *Understanding End Times Prophecy*, 219.

11. Archer, "Mid-Seventieth Week Rapture," 142.

12. Robert L. Thomas, *Revelation 8–22: An Exegetical Commentary* (Chicago: Moody, 1995), 220. John MacArthur's view of the harvest seems best: "The grain harvest symbolizes the seven bowl judgments, the grape harvest the judgment of Armageddon." John MacArthur, *Revelation 12–22* (Chicago: Moody, 2000), 111.

13. J. Daniel Hays, J. Scott Duvall, and C. Marvin Pate, *Dictionary of Biblical Prophecy and End Times* (Grand Rapids: Zondervan, 2007), 286.

14. John Piper, "Definitions and Observations Concerning the Second Coming of Christ," *Desiring God*, August 30, 1987, http://www.desiringgod.org/articles/definitions-and-observations-concerning-the-second-coming-of-christ.

15. Piper, "Definitions and Observations."

16. Robert H. Gundry, *The Church and the Tribulation* (Grand Rapids: Zondervan, 1973), 135.

17. Piper, "Definitions and Observations."

18. Piper, "Definitions and Observations."

19. Charles C. Ryrie, *Come Quickly, Lord Jesus* (Eugene, OR: Harvest House, 1996), 97. To avoid this obvious difficulty for the postrib view Robert Gundry is "forced" to move the judgment of the sheep and the goats to the end of the millennium and equate it with the Great White Throne judgment in Revelation 20:11-15. Robert Gundry, *The Church and the Tribulation* (Grand Rapids: Zondervan, 1973), 166. Ryrie refutes Gundry's view very effectively (Ryrie, *Come Quickly, Lord Jesus*, 98-101).

20. John F. Walvoord, *The Rapture Question*, rev. ed. (Grand Rapids: Zondervan, 1979), 268.

21. Gerald B. Stanton, *Kept from the Hour* (Miami Springs, FL: Schoettle, 1991), 166.

22. John MacArthur & Richard Mayhue, gen. eds., *Christ's Prophetic Plan* (Chicago: Moody, 2012), 88.

23. Marvin Rosenthal, *The Pre-Wrath Rapture of the Church* (Nashville: Thomas Nelson, 1990), 59.

24. Rosenthal, *The Pre-Wrath Rapture of the Church*, 60.

25. Rosenthal, *The Pre-Wrath Rapture of the Church*, 112-13.

26. Paul Feinberg, *The Rapture: Pre-, Mid-, or Post-Tribulational?* (Grand Rapids: Zondervan, 1984), 223.

27. Benware, *Understanding End Times Prophecy*, 220.

28. Ryrie, *Come Quickly, Lord Jesus*, 24-25.

Chapter 5: History of the Rapture Doctrine

1. Michael F. Bird, *Evangelical Theology* (Grand Rapids: Zondervan, 2013), 300. Cf. also Ben Witherington III, *The Problem of Evangelical Theology* (Waco, TX: Baylor University, 2005), 94-96.

2. Cf. Donald Fairburn, "Contemporary Millennial/Tribulational Debates: Whose Side Was the Early Church On?" in C.L. Blomberg and J.W. Chung, *A Case for Historic Premillennialism* (Grand Rapids: Baker, 2009), 128. Such opinions often lack any serious interaction with the plethora of materials available from English authors of the seventeenth and eighteenth centuries.

3. William Watson, *Dispensationalism Before Darby* (Silverton, OR: Lampion Press, 2015), 339. Cf. Paul Boyer, *When Time Shall Be No More* (Cambridge, MA: Harvard University, 1994), 88.

4. Thomas Ice, "A History of the Rapture Teaching," in Tim LaHaye, Thomas Ice, and Ed Hindson, eds. *Popular Handbook on the Rapture* (Eugene, OR: Harvest House, 2011), 59.

5. Norman Geisler, *Systematic Theology* (Minneapolis: Bethany House, 2005), 4:632.

6. *The Ante-Nicene Fathers* (Grand Rapids: Eerdmans, 1985), 558.

7. Larry Crutchfield, "Early Church Fathers and the Foundations of Dispensationalism," Part VI, *The Conservative Theological Digest* (3.9; August 1999), 194.

8. J. Barton Payne, *The Imminent Appearing of Christ* (Grand Rapids: Eerdmans, 1962), 102. Quoted at length by Ice, "A History of the Rapture Teaching," 64.

9. Quoted in Geisler, *Systematic Theology*, 567-70.

10. Francis X. Gumerlock, "The Rapture in the Apocalypse of Elijah," *Bibliotheca Sacra* (October-December, 2013), 418-31.

11. English translation from *The Apocalypse of Elijah: Based on P. Chester Beatty* (Ithaca, NY: Scholar's Press, 1981), 56-57.

12. Gumerlock, "The Rapture in the Apocalypse of Elijah," 422.

13. Francis X. Gumerlock, "Apocalyptic Spirituality in the Early Middle Ages: Hope for Escaping the Fire of Doomsday through a Pre-Conflagration Rapture," in G.S. Weaver and I.H. Clary, eds. *The Pure Flame of Devotion: The History of Christian Spirituality* (Guelph, ON: Joshua Press, 2013), 101-14.

14. Paul Alexander, *The Byzantine Apocalyptic Tradition* (Berkeley: University of California, 1985), 210. He considers the Pseudo-Ephraem quotation to refer to a pretribulational rapture and calls it "one of the most interesting apocalyptic texts of the early Middle Ages."

15. An English translation of the entire sermon can be found at www.pre-trib .org/article-view.php?id=169.

16. See details in Thomas Ice, "A History of the Rapture Teaching," 65-68. Cf. also Francis Gumerlock, "A Rapture Citation in the Fourteenth Century," *Bibliotheca Sacra* (vol. 159, no 635; July-September, 2002), 349-62.

17. John Calvin, *1 and 2 Thessalonians*, Alister McGrath and J.I. Packer, eds. (Wheaton, IL: Crossway, 1999), 49. Emphasis added.

18. John Bale, "The Image of Both Churches," in *Select Works of Bishop Bale* (London: Parker Society, 1849). For a modern version cf. Gretchen Minton, ed. *John Bale's the Image of Both Churches* (New York: Springer, 2013).

19. Minton, "Appendix 4: Periods of History and Symbols in the *Image*," 489-92. She points out that Bale overlaps the seven ages of history from Adam to Christ upon the seven ages since Christ.

20. Osiander was a close friend and associate of Copernicus and wrote the preface to his *De Revolution Orbium Colestium*, in which Copernicus set forth the heliocentric theory.

21. K.R. Firth, *The Apocalyptic Tradition in Reformation Britain 1530–1645* (Oxford: Oxford University Press, 1979), 63.

22. See R. Bauckham, *Tudor Apocalypse* (Appleford: Courtenay Classics, 1978), 45-51.

23. Cf. Paul Christianson, *Reformers and Babylon* (Toronto: University of Toronto Press, 1978), 97; R. Clouse, John Napier and Apocalyptic Thought," *Sixteenth Century Journal*, V (1974), 101-14; W. Ball, *A Great Expectation: Eschatological Thought in English Protestantism to 1600* (Leiden: E.J. Brill, 1975), 59-82.

24. Firth, *The Apocalyptic Tradition in Reformation Britain 1530–1645*, 191-99.

25. Broughton's works were collected under the title *The Works of the Great Albionean Divine, Renowned in Many Nations for Rare Skill in Salems and Athens Tongues* (London: 1662). Cf. M. Reeves, *The Influence of Prophecy in the Later Middle Ages* (Oxford: Clarendon Press, 1969), 271-82. Christianson, *The Apocalyptic Tradition in Reformation Britain 1530–1645*, 107-09, comments on Broughton's date, "He could still be right!" He was the only ancient date-setter who has yet to be proven wrong.

26. For a collection of his writings, see *The Workes of Thomas Brightman* (London: 1644). Cf. also P. Toon, ed. *Puritan Eschatology* (London: James Clark, 1970), 26-32; R. Clouse, "The Apocalyptic Interpretation of Thomas Brightman and Joseph Mede," *Bulletin of the Evangelical Theological Society*, XI (1968), 181-93.

27. Brightman, *A Revelation of the Revelation*, 322-27; 480-88.

28. Brightman, *A Revelation of the Revelation*, 559.

29. J.H. Alsted, *Tractus de Mille Annis* (Herborn, 1618), later issued as *Diatribe De Milleannis Apocalypticus* (Frankfurt, 1627); and translated into English by W. Burton as *The Beloved City: or, the Saints Reign on Earth a Thousand Yeares* (London: 1643).

30. See Christopher Hill, *Antichrist in Seventeenth-Century England* (London: Oxford University, 1971), 28-31.

31. Firth, *The Apocalyptic Tradition in Reformation Britain 1530–1645*, 215-18.

32. Thomas Goodwin, "An Exposition of Ephesians," in *Works of Thomas Goodwin* (Edinburgh: 1861–1864). For a survey of Goodwin's views see Tai Liu, *Discord in Zion* (The Hague: Martinus Nijhoff, 1973), 1-28; and G.F. Nuttal,

Visible Saints: The Congregational Way 1640–1660 (Oxford: Oxford University Press, 1957).

33. The authorship of this message is debated. P. Toon, *Puritan Eschatology 1600–1660* (Cambridge: James Clarke, 1970), Appendix I, makes a convincing argument for Goodwin.

34. Watson, *Dispensationalism Before Darby*, 129.

35. Thomas Manton, *Meate Out of the Eater or Hopes of Unity in and by Divided and Distracted Times* (London: 1647), 2-13.

36. William Sherwin, *Eirenikon: or a Peaceable Consideration of Christ's Peaceful Kingdom on Earth to Come* (np, 1665), 4-8; and *Exanstasis, or the Saints Rising* (London: 1674), 43-45.

37. Cited in Craig Blaising and Darrell Bock, *Progressive Dispensationalism* (Grand Rapids: Baker, 1993), 118.

38. Peter Jurieu, *The Accomplishment of the Scripture Prophecies, or the Approaching Deliverance of the Church* (London: 1687), 308.

39. Pierre Poiret, *The Divine Œconomy: or An Universal System of the Works and Purposes of God Towards Men* (London: 1713), 4.150.

40. William Penn, *A Brief Account of the Rise and Progress of the People Called Quakers* (London: 1695), 13-15.

41. John Edwards, *A Complete History or Survey of All the Dispensations and Methods of Religion* (London: 1699), vol. 1.

42. Watson, *Dispensationalism Before Darby*, 129.

43. Watson, *Dispensationalism Before Darby*, 177.

44. Watson, *Dispensationalism Before Darby*, 136-37.

45. Barton Holyday, *Three Sermons upon the Passion, Resurrection, and Ascension of Our Savior* (London: 1626).

46. Thomas Draxe, *The Lamb's Spouse: Or the Heavenly Bride—a Theological Discourse* (London: 1608), D4.

47. Joseph Mede, *Works of Joseph Mede*, iv, 775-76.

48. Watson, *Dispensationalism Before Darby*, 138-40.

49. John Archer, *The Personall Reign of Christ Upon Earth* (London: 1642), 16-19.

50. Watson, *Dispensationalism Before Darby*, 141-142. Cf. Ephraim Huit, *The Whole Prophecie of Daniel Explained* (London: 1643), 196-99.

51. Watson, *Dispensationalism Before Darby*, 144.

52. E. Avery, *Scripture-Prophecies Opened* (London: 1647), 7-8.

53. Nathaniel Holmes, *Apocalypsis Anastaseos: The Resurrection Revealed* (London: 1653), 492-94.

54. Watson, *Dispensationalism Before Darby*, 149-51. John Browne, *A Brief Survey of the Prophetical and Evangelical Events of the Last Times* (London: 1654), 1-46.

55. William Sherwin, *Eirenikon: or a Peaceful Consideration of Christ's Peaceful Kingdom on Earth* (np., 1665), 40-43.

56. Watson, *Dispensationalism Before Darby*, 157-58.

57. Watson, *Dispensationalism Before Darby*, 157.

58. Thomas Vincent, *Christ's Certain and Sudden Appearance to Judgment* (London: 1667), 53-54.

59. Watson, *Dispensationalism Before Darby*, 159-60. Samuel Hutchinson, *Declaration of a Future Glorious Estate of the Church* (London: 1667), 8-9.

60. J[oshua] S[prigg], *News of a New World from the Word and Works of God* (London: 1676), 8-9.

61. Sprigg, *News of a New World*, 132-38.

62. Watson, *Dispensationalism Before Darby*, 165-66.

63. Watson, *Dispensationalism Before Darby*, 176.

64. [William Lloyd], *An Exposition of the Prophecy of Seventy Weeks* (np, 1690).

65. Watson, *Dispensationalism Before Darby*, 243.

66. Increase Mather, *The Blessed Hope, and the Glorious Appearing of the Great God Our Saviour, Jesus Christ* (Boston: 1701), 22, 33, 122, 131.

67. Morgan Edwards, *Two Accidental Exercises on Subjects Bearing the Following Titles: Millennium, Last Novelties* (Philadelphia: 1788; written in c. 1743), 7.

68. Jonathan Edwards, *A History of the Work of Redemption* (New York: American Tract Society, 1808; first published in 1774), 420-21.

69. Watson, *Dispensationalism Before Darby*, 262. He also includes examples from Killingsworth, Broughton, Hardy, and Fraser.

Chapter 6: The Rapture and the Return

1. Glenn R. Kreider, "The Rapture and the Day of the Lord," in *Evidence for the Rapture: A Biblical Case for Pretribulationism*, gen. ed. John F. Hart (Chicago: Moody, 2015), 83.

2. Alan Bandy and Benjamin Merkle, *Understanding Prophecy* (Grand Rapids: Kregel, 2015), 191-212.

3. Kreider, "The Rapture and the Day of the Lord," 83.

4. Charles C. Ryrie, *Come Quickly, Lord Jesus* (Eugene, OR: Harvest House, 1996), 47.

5. Ryrie, *Come Quickly, Lord Jesus*, 47-48.

6. George Eldon Ladd, *The Blessed Hope* (Grand Rapids: Wm. B. Eerdmans, 1989), 69-70.

7. Gleason L. Archer Jr., *The Rapture: Pre-, Mid-, or Post-Tribulational?* (Grand Rapids: Zondervan, 1984), 216.

8. Archer Jr., *The Rapture*.

9. Kreider, "The Rapture and the Day of the Lord," 83-84.

10. Ryrie, *Come Quickly, Lord Jesus*, 51.

11. Douglas J. Moo, *The Rapture: Pre-, Mid-, or Post-Tribulational?* (Grand Rapids: Zondervan, 1984), 177.

12. John F. Walvoord, *The Rapture Question*, rev. ed. (Grand Rapids: Zondervan, 1979), 94.

13. Paul D. Feinberg, *The Rapture: Pre-, Mid-, or Post-Tribulational?* (Grand Rapids: Zondervan, 1984), 80-85. Paul N. Benware, *Understanding End Times Prophecy* (Chicago: Moody, 1995), 206. Walvoord also lists important contrasts between the translation (rapture) and the second coming. Walvoord, *The Rapture Question*, 93-94.

14. Paul N. Benware, *Understanding End Times Prophecy* (Chicago: Moody, 1995), 207.

15. George Eldon Ladd, *The Blessed Hope* (Grand Rapids: Eerdmans, 1990), 91.

16. Ladd, *The Blessed Hope*, 91-92.

17. Moo, *The Rapture: Pre-, Mid-, or Post-Tribulational?*, 98. Moo addresses a few

of the suggested omissions of details in rapture passages that are missing from return passages and vice versa (98-101).

18. Moo, *The Rapture: Pre-, Mid-, or Post-Tribulational?*, 98. The problem with taking Matthew 24:31 as a reference to the rapture is that, as Moo admits, no rapture of living believers to heaven is stated in the verse. Also, at the rapture event there will not only be the rapture of living believers, there will also be a resurrection of deceased Christians. No specific mention of either a rapture or resurrection is found in Matthew 24:31. All this is referencing is a gathering of the elect. Moreover, the entire context of Matthew 24 is Jewish, indicating that the "elect" in Matthew 24:31 are Jewish believers alive on earth at Christ's coming who are gathered from the four corners of the earth.

19. Moo, *The Rapture: Pre-, Mid-, or Post-Tribulational?*, 99.

20. Moo, *The Rapture: Pre-, Mid-, or Post-Tribulational?*, 100-01.

21. John MacArthur, *The Second Coming* (Wheaton, IL: Crossway, 1999), 87.

Chapter 7: Bringing the Future into Focus

1. Charles C. Ryrie, *Basic Theology* (Wheaton, IL: Victor, 1986), 439-40.

2. There is a fifth approach that some have adopted recently known as the eclectic view. This is a newer approach to Revelation that attempts to combine the strengths of the four other views while avoiding or at least minimizing their weaknesses. J. Daniel Hays, J. Scott Duvall, and C. Marvin Pate, *Dictionary of Biblical Prophecy and End Times* (Grand Rapids: Zondervan, 2007), 128. The eclectic view is enjoying increasing support among scholars. Some who have embraced this view are Greg Beale, G.R. Beasley-Murray, Alan Johnson, Dennis E. Johnson, and Craig Keener. See Grant R. Osborne, *Revelation*, Baker Exegetical Commentary of the New Testament, ed. Moises Silva (Grand Rapids: Baker Academic, 2002), 21. Eclectics acknowledge that some parts of Revelation await fulfillment in the end times. "Although opinions vary about which elements have been fulfilled and which elements are still future, most agree that Revelation 19–22 awaits fulfillment. God's ultimate victory over the forces of evil will be decisively demonstrated in history." J. Daniel Hays, J. Scott Duvall, and C. Marvin Pate, *Dictionary of Biblical Prophecy and End Times* (Grand Rapids: Zondervan, 2007), 129. George Eldon Ladd is an eclectic who blends the preterist and futurist approaches. George Eldon Ladd, *A Commentary on the Revelation of John* (Grand Rapids: Eerdmans, 1972), 14. In spite of the claim to be blended, most eclectic scholars heavily emphasize the idealist or spiritual approach.

3. R.C. Sproul, *The Last Days According to Jesus* (Grand Rapids: Baker, 1998), 228.

4. Sproul, *The Last Days According to Jesus*, 24.

5. David Chilton, *The Days of Vengeance: An Exposition of the Book of Revelation* (Tyler, TX: Dominion Press, 1987), 40.

6. R.C. Sproul, *The Last Days According to Jesus*, 158.

7. Grant R. Osborne, *Revelation*, Baker Exegetical Commentary of the New Testament, ed. Moises Silva (Grand Rapids: Baker Academic, 2002), 20. Greg Beale notes that the background for Revelation is the prophecies of Daniel that deal with the nations of the earth. He says, "A closely related problem is that these preterist interpreters understand the prophecies of final judgment in Revelation to be limited to Israel, whereas Daniel 2 and 7 anticipate a universal judgment. John's depictions, including his allusions to Daniel, are best interpreted in the same way as Daniel. Consequently, the burden of proof rests on these preterists to provide an exegetical rationale for both exchanging a pagan nation with Israel as the primary object of Daniel's final judgment and for limiting the last judgment mainly to Israel and not apply it universally." G.K. Beale, *The Book of Revelation*, The New International Greek New Testament, ed. I. Howard Marshall and Donald A. Hagner (Grand Rapids: Eerdmans, 1999), 45.

8. For a detailed presentation defending the AD 95 date of Revelation, go to pretrib.org, where a copy of my (Mark) doctoral dissertation from Dallas Seminary is available. The title of the dissertation is "A Defense of the Domitianic Date of the Book of the Book of Revelation." At the website you can also view a debate on the date of Revelation between myself and Hank Hanegraaff that was held in December 2007 in Dallas, Texas.

9. Osborne, *Revelation*, 18.

10. G.K. Beale, *The Book of Revelation*, The New International Greek New Testament, ed. I. Howard Marshall and Donald A. Hagner (Grand Rapids: Eerdmans, 1999), 46.

11. J. Daniel Hays, J. Scott Duvall, and C. Marvin Pate, *Dictionary of Biblical Prophecy and End Times* (Grand Rapids: Zondervan, 2007), 201.

12. Hays, Duvall, and Pate, *Dictionary of Biblical Prophecy and End Times*, 202.

13. Robert L. Thomas, *Revelation 1–7: An Exegetical Commentary* (Chicago: Moody, 1992), 31.

14. Dennis E. Johnson, *Triumph of the Lamb* (Phillipsburg, NJ: P&R Publishing, 2001), 360.

15. Paige Patterson, *Revelation*, The New American Commentary, gen. ed. E. Ray Clendenen, vol. 39 (Nashville: B&H Publishing, 2012), 28.

16. Hays, Duvall, and Pate, *Dictionary of Biblical Prophecy and End Times*, 172.

17. Beale, *The Book of Revelation*, 47.

18. Steve Gregg, ed., *Revelation: Four Views, a Parallel Commentary* (Nashville: Thomas Nelson, 1997), 459.

19. Gregg, *Revelation: Four Views, a Parallel Commentary*.

20. Philip Schaff, *History of the Christian Church*, vol. 2 (Grand Rapids: Eerdmans Publishing Company, 1973), 614.

21. Gregg, *Revelation*, 458-59.

Chapter 8: Is the Rapture Imminent?

1. Mark Bailey, "The Doctrine of the Future," in D.J. Bingham and G.R. Kreider, eds. *Eschatology* (Grand Rapids: Kregel, 2016), 395.

2. Gerald Stanton, *Kept from the Hour* (Haysville, NC: Schoettle, 1991), 108.

3. Robert H. Gundry, *The Church and the Tribulation* (Grand Rapids: Zondervan, 1973), 29. Emphasis in the original.

4. John A. Sproule, *In Defense of Pretribulationism* (Winona Lake, IN: BMH Books, 1980), 12.

5. Renald Showers, *Maranatha Our Lord, Come!* (Bellmawr, NJ: Friends of Israel, 1995), 127.

6. Wayne Brindle, "The Doctrine of an Imminent Rapture," in Tim LaHaye, Thomas Ice, and Ed Hindson, eds. *The Popular Handbook on the Rapture* (Eugene, OR: Harvest House, 2011), 77.

7. Marvin J. Rosenthal, "Imminence: Does the Bible Teach an Any-Moment Rapture?," *Zion's Fire Magazine*, August/September 1990, http://www.zion shope.org/zionsfire/articles/imminence.html.

8. Rosenthal, "Imminence."

9. Thomas Ice, "Differences Between the Rapture and the Second Coming," Pre-Trib.org, 3, accessed at http://www.pre-trib.org/data/pdf/Ice-Differences BetweenTheRapt.pdf.

10. Ice, "Differences," 4.

11. Rosenthal, "Imminence."

12. Todd Strandberg, "Imminency," RaptureReady.com, http://www.rapture ready.com/imminency/.

13. LaHaye, Tim. *Revelation Unveiled* (Kindle Locations 1813-1816). Zondervan. Kindle Edition.

14. LaHaye, *Revelation Unveiled* (Kindle Locations 1836-1842).

15. Mark Hitchcock, *The End* (Carol Stream, IL: Tyndale, 2012), 136.

16. F. Kenton Beshore and R. William Keller, *When? When Will the Rapture Take Place?* (Costa Mesa, CA: World Bible Society, 2011), 152.

17. Wayne Brindle, "Biblical Evidence for the Imminence of the Rapture," *Bibliotheca Sacra*, 158 no 630 Ap-Je 2001, pp. 138-51. Accessed at http://www .pre-trib.org/data/pdf/Brindle-BiblicalEvidenceforth.pdf.

18. Robert Dean, Jr., "Three Foundational Rapture Passages," Pre-Trib.org, 10-11. Accessed at http://www.pre-trib.org/data/pdf/Dean-TheThreeMajor Rapture.pdf.

19. Paul D. Feinberg, "The Case for the Pretribulation Rapture Position," in *Three Views on the Rapture* (Grand Rapids: Zondervan, 1996), 80.

20. Adapted from Ed Hindson, "The Rapture and Glorious Appearing of Jesus Christ," Pre-Trib.org. Accessed at http://www.pre-trib.org/articles/view/ rapture-and-glorious-appearing-of-jesus-christ.

Chapter 9: Not Destined for Wrath

1. The partial rapture view holds that only believers who are prepared, ready, and faithful will be raptured before the tribulation while those left behind on earth will endure all or part of the wrath of the tribulation.

2. Paul D. Feinberg, *The Rapture: Pre-, Mid-, or Post-Tribulational?* (Grand Rapids: Zondervan, 1984), 223.

3. Paul N. Benware, *Understanding End Times Prophecy* (Chicago: Moody, 1995), 171.

4. Feinberg, *The Rapture: Pre-, Mid-, or Post-Tribulational?*, 58.

5. George Eldon Ladd, *The Blessed Hope* (Grand Rapids: Eerdmans, 1956), 129.

6. Robert H. Gundry, *The Church and the Tribulation* (Grand Rapids: Zondervan, 1973), 63.

7. Feinberg, *The Rapture: Pre-, Mid-, or Post-Tribulational?*, 62.

8. In Revelation, there are 3 series of 7 judgments—the seals, trumpets, and bowls. This, of course, equals a total of 21. But because the seventh seal contains the 7 trumpets and the seventh trumpet contains the 7 bowls, the total number of specific judgments is actually 19 rather than 21.

9. John F. Walvoord, *The Rapture Question*, rev. ed. (Grand Rapids: Zondervan, 1979), 225.

10. J.F. Strombeck, *First the Rapture* (Moline, IL: Strombeck Agency, 1950; reprint, Grand Rapids: Kregel, 1992), 133.

11. Benware, *Understanding End Times Prophecy*, 174.

12. C.F. Hogg and W.E. Vine, *The Epistles to the Thessalonians* (Fincastle, VA: Scripture Truth, 1959), 48.

13. D. Edmond Hiebert, *1 & 2 Thessalonians*, rev. ed. (Chicago: Moody, 1992), 211.

14. Renald Showers, *Maranatha: Our Lord, Come!* (Bellmawr, NJ: Friends of Israel Gospel Ministry, 1995), 194.

15. John MacArthur, *1 & 2 Thessalonians* (Chicago: Moody, 2002), 29.

16. Gary S. Shogren, *1 & 2 Thessalonians*, Exegetical Commentary on the New Testament, gen. ed. Clinton E. Arnold (Grand Rapids: Zondervan, 2012), 75-76.

17. Shogren, *1 & 2 Thessalonians*, 76.

18. Gleason L. Archer, Jr., *The Rapture: Pre-, Mid-, or Post-Tribulational?* (Grand Rapids: Zondervan, 1984), 117-18.

19. Charles C. Ryrie, *First & Second Thessalonians*, Everyman's Bible Commentary (Chicago: Moody, 2001), 72.

20. Mike Stallard, *The Books of First & Second Thessalonians*, Twenty-First Century Biblical Commentary Series, gen. eds. Mal Couch and Ed Hindson (Chattanooga, TN: AMG Publishers, 2009), 96.

21. John F. Walvoord, *The Thessalonian Epistles* (Grand Rapids: Zondervan, n.d.), 54.

22. Paul Feinberg provides an excellent, thorough discussion of the usage of *ek* in the Septuagint and the New Testament and *tereo ek* in John 17:15 in Paul D. Feinberg, *The Rapture: Pre-, Mid-, or Post-Tribulational?* (Grand Rapids, MI: Zondervan, 1984), 63-71.

23. Richard Mayhue, *Christ's Prophetic Plan*, gen. eds. John MacArthur and Richard Mayhue (Chicago: Moody, 2012), 96.

24. Charles C. Ryrie, *Come Quickly, Lord Jesus* (Eugene, OR: Harvest House, 1996), 136. Thomas makes the same argument that any of these other prepositions would have made the meaning more obvious. Robert L. Thomas, *Revelation 1–7: An Exegetical Commentary* (Chicago: Moody, 1992), 286.

25. Daniel Green, "Revelation," in *The Moody Bible Commentary*, gen. eds. Michael Rydelnik and Michael Vanlaningham (Chicago: Moody, 2014), 2006.

26. Believers on earth during the tribulation in Revelation 6–18 are not the church, but those who come to faith in Jesus after the rapture. These believers, often called tribulation saints, aren't promised exemption from God's eschatological wrath as is the church.

27. Andrew M. Woods, "John and the Rapture: Revelation 2-3," in *Evidence for the Rapture*, gen. ed. John F. Hart (Chicago: Moody, 2015), 198.

28. Feinberg, *The Rapture: Pre-, Mid-, or Post-Tribulational?*, 70.

29. Andrew M. Woods, "John and the Rapture: Revelation 2-3," 199.

30. Showers, *Maranatha: Our Lord, Come!*, 211-12.

31. Norman L. Geisler, *Systematic Theology*, vol. 4 (Minneapolis: Bethany, 2004), 654.

32. Thomas, *Revelation 1–7*, 288.

33. Thomas, *Revelation 1–7*, 290.

34. Benware, *Understanding End Times Prophecy*, 175.

35. Ryrie, *Come Quickly, Lord Jesus*, 137-38.

Chapter 10: The Necessity of an Interval Between the Rapture and the Return

1. John F. Walvoord, *The Rapture Question*, rev. ed. (Grand Rapids: Zondervan, 1979), 83.

2. Paul N. Benware, *Understanding End Times Prophecy* (Chicago: Moody, 1995), 181.

3. Benware, *Understanding End Times Prophecy*, 182.

4. Posttribulationist George Eldon Ladd says there is no evidence in Scripture that believers will be rewarded before Christ returns. George Eldon Ladd, *The Blessed Hope* (Grand Rapids: Eerdmans, 1986), 103. Ladd's assertion overlooks Revelation 19, which says the rewarded bride is in heaven with Christ before He returns to earth.

5. Ladd, *The Blessed Hope*, 103.

6. Walvoord, *The Rapture Question*, rev. ed., 85.

7. Ladd, *The Blessed Hope*, 99-100.

8. Ryrie, *Come Quickly, Lord Jesus* (Eugene, OR: Harvest House, 1996), 90.

9. John MacArthur and Richard Mayhue, *Biblical Doctrine* (Wheaton, IL: Crossway, 2017), 900.

10. Robert H. Gundry, *The Church and the Tribulation* (Grand Rapids: Zondervan, 1973), 163-71.

11. Gundry, *The Church and the Tribulation*, 167-68.

12. Ryrie, *Come Quickly, Lord Jesus*, 101.

13. Paul D. Feinberg, *The Rapture: Pre-, Mid-, or Post-Tribulational?* (Grand Rapids: Zondervan, 1984), 77.

14. D.A. Carson, "Matthew," in *The Expositor's Bible Commentary*, gen. ed. Frank E. Gaebelein, vol. 8 (Grand Rapids: Zondervan, 1984), 521.

15. This issue is pertinent only to premillennialists—that is, those who believe in a literal, earthly, future 1,000-year reign of Christ. Amillennial posttribulationists, who deny a future millennium, have no need to populate a literal kingdom, so this argument poses no issue for them.

16. Walvoord, *The Rapture Question*, 86-87.

17. Ryrie, *Come Quickly, Lord Jesus*, 88.

18. Ryrie gives an explanation for the posttribulationists' avoidance of this issue: "This may be because they do not usually put the details of their system together in an orderly way. Their picture of the future is painted with broad strokes, not fine detail. Posttribulationists do not sponsor prophecy

conferences in which their speakers are expected to describe rather specifically the system they promote. As a result, some posttribulationists may not have thought about this question." Ryrie, *Come Quickly, Lord Jesus*, 88-89.

19. Gundry, *The Church and the Tribulation*, 167, emphasis in original. In his search for millennial parents to populate the kingdom, Gundry also proposes that the 144,000 Jews won't be saved until the very end of Christ's return as they look on Him as He returns in glory (82-83). He says, "They are converted immediately after the rapture as they see their Messiah descending onto the earth...and entering the millennium in their natural bodies to form the nucleus of the reestablished Davidic kingdom" (82). We reject the view that the 144,000 will be unsaved throughout the entire tribulation. At the beginning of their ministry, they are sealed by God on their foreheads and called "the bondservants of our God" (Revelation 7:3), which is a strange description for them if they are unbelievers. How can one be a bondservant of God and unredeemed? Nevertheless, even if this view about the 144,000 is correct, we know that there will also be Gentiles in the kingdom in non-glorified bodies, so Gundry solves only half the problem.

20. Ryrie, *Come Quickly, Lord Jesus*, 95.

21. Feinberg, *The Rapture: Pre-, Mid-, or Post-Tribulational?*, 79.

Chapter 11: Does It Really Matter?

1. Gerry Breshears and Mark Driscoll, *Vintage Church* (Wheaton, IL: Crossway, 2008), 61.

2. This is clearly emphasized by Andreas Köstenberger, Darrell Bock, and Josh Chatraw, *Truth in a Culture of Doubt* (Nashville: B&H, 2014). They point out that theological biases often lead to "unduly skeptical conclusions."

3. See the detailed discussion of the "Timing of Satan's Binding" in Matt Waymeyer, *Amillennialism and the Age to Come* (The Woodlands, TX: Kress Biblical Resources, 2016), 175-206. He provides a premillennial critique of the amillennial view, noting that the absolute confinement of Satan described in Revelation 20 is not a present reality and, therefore, must be a future event that will follow the return of Christ as described in Revelation 19.

4. Cf. Sam Storms, *Kingdom Come: The Amillennial Alternative* (Ross-Shire, Scotland: Mentor, 2013); Kim Riddlebarger, *A Case for Amillennialism* (Grand Rapids: Baker, 2013).

5. Jeffery Bingham and Glenn Kreider, eds. *Eschatology* (Grand Rapids: Kregel, 2016).

6. For example, Burge's claim that "dispensationalism embraced a pessimistic view of history…calling sinners to repent and be saved from the inevitable catastrophe of the human story" hardly seems appropriate because all evangelical views of eschatology are ultimately calling sinners to repent and be saved from some kind of inevitable final judgment. See Gary Burge, "Why I Am Not a Christian Zionist," quoted in Kreider, 355.

7. Michael Bird, *Evangelical Theology* (Grand Rapids: Zondervan, 2013), 235. A self-described "historic premillennialist," Bird raises a number of significant issues that are important to all eschatological views.

8. Alan Bandy and Benjamin Merkle, *Understanding Prophecy* (Grand Rapids: Kregel, 2015), 67. For a more popularized approach cf. Justin Buzzard, *The Big Story* (Chicago: Moody, 2013).

9. The affirmation of the second coming of Christ is stated in virtually all Christian confessions of faith: Catholic, Orthodox, Protestant, Anglican, Presbyterian, Baptist, Methodist, Lutheran, etc.

10. See the insightful comments of Richard Mouw, "This World Is Not My Home," *Christianity Today* (April 24, 2006), 86-90.

11. Charles Ryrie, *Dispensationalism Today* (Chicago: Moody, 1965), 43.

12. John Feinberg, ed. *Continuity and Discontinuity* (Chicago: Moody, 1988), 73.

13. Michael Vlach, "What Is Dispensationalism?" in John MacArthur and Richard Mayhue, eds., *Christ's Prophetic Plans* (Chicago: Moody, 2012), 22. Cf. also nonpremillennialist J. Richard Middleton, *A New Heaven and a New Earth* (Grand Rapids: Baker, 2014). Middleton wrestles with the relation of the obviously physical descriptions of the spiritual aspects of God's redemptive purpose.

14. Philip Ryken, *Christian Worldview: A Student's Guide* (Wheaton, IL: Crossway, 2013), 17.

15. Barry Horner, *Future Israel* (Nashville: B&H, 2009), xviii. He quotes Steven Sizer and Colin Chapman.

16. Horner, *Future Israel*, xix.

17. Horner, *Future Israel*, 331. Cf. also Tim LaHaye and Ed Hindson, *Target Israel* (Eugene, OR: Harvest House, 2015), 39-66.

18. Walter Elwell, ed. *Evangelical Dictionary of Biblical Theology* (Grand Rapids: Baker, 1997), 1273.

19. Karl Barth, *Church Dogmatics* (London: Continuum, 2004, 1932), 1.1:11.

20. Bird, *Evangelical Theology*, 30-31. He follows the analogy of Kevin Vanhoozer, *Drama of Doctrine* (Louisville: John Knox, 2005), 72. Emphasis in original.

21. Critics of the pretribulational view often mislabel it as "doom and gloom" theology. Cf. Richard Abanes, *End-Time Visions* (Nashville: B&H, 1998), 303-325. While Abanes provides ample details about overspeculation and prophetic sensationalizing, he lumps occult doomsayers, apocalyptic cult leaders, and Christian prophecy teachers in the same category.

22. Richard Mayhue, "Why a Pre-Tribulation Rapture?" in John MacArthur and Richard Mayhue, eds. *Christ's Prophetic Plans* (Chicago: Moody, 2012), 97.

Chapter 12: Are You Ready?

1. David Jeremiah, *Is This the End?* (Nashville: W Publishing, 2016), xi.

2. See E. Hindson, "Isaiah," in E. Hindson and W. Kroll, eds. *King James Bible Commentary* (Nashville: Thomas Nelson, 1983), 1335-38, 1350-51.

OTHER BIBLE PROPHECY BOOKS
BY HARVEST HOUSE PUBLISHERS

101 Answers to Questions About the Book of Revelation
Mark Hitchcock

15 Future Events that Will Shake the World / Ed Hindson

40 Days Through Daniel / Ron Rhodes

40 Days Through Revelation / Ron Rhodes

The Amazing Claims of Bible Prophecy / Mark Hitchcock

As It Was in the Days of Noah / Jeff Kinley

Bible Prophecy Answer Book / Ron Rhodes

Charting the Bible Chronologically
Ed Hindson and Thomas Ice

Charting the End Times / Tim LaHaye and Thomas Ice

The End of America? / Jeff Kinley

The End Times in Chronological Order / Ron Rhodes

Exploring Bible Prophecy from Genesis to Revelation
Tim LaHaye and Ed Hindson

ISIS, Iran, Israel and the End of Days / Mark Hitchcock

Israel on High Alert / Ron Rhodes

Middle East Burning / Mark Hitchcock

The Popular Encyclopedia of Bible Prophecy
Tim LaHaye and Ed Hindson

Target Israel / Tim LaHaye and Ed Hindson

The Topical Handbook About Bible Prophecy / Ron Rhodes

Who Is the Antichrist? / Mark Hitchcock

To learn more about Harvest House books and
to read sample chapters, visit our website:

www.harvesthousepublishers.com

HARVEST HOUSE PUBLISHERS
EUGENE, OREGON